The Novel Experience

signale minima

Series Editor: Paul Fleming, Cornell University

Elegantly concise books that capture urgent, experimental, occasional, or quirky ideas within German studies and humanistic thought.

The Novel Experience

*Reading Fiction with Nāgārjuna,
Nietzsche, and William James*

HELMUT MÜLLER-SIEVERS

A Signale Book

Cornell University Press and Cornell University Library
Ithaca and London

Cornell University Press and Cornell University Library
gratefully acknowledge the College of Arts & Sciences,
Cornell University, for support of the Signale series.

First published 2025 by Cornell University Press and
Cornell University Library

Library of Congress Cataloging-in-Publication Data
Names: Müller-Sievers, Helmut author
Title: The novel experience : reading fiction with
    Nāgārjuna, Nietzsche, and William James / Helmut
    Müller-Sievers.
Description: Ithaca : Cornell University Press, 2025. |
    "A Signale book" | Includes bibliographical references.
Identifiers: LCCN 2025019670 (print) |
    LCCN 2025019671 (ebook) | ISBN 9781501785627
    hardcover | ISBN 9781501785634 paperback |
    ISBN 9781501785658 epub | ISBN 9781501785641 pdf
Subjects: LCSH: Fiction—History and criticism—Theory,
    etc. | Reader-response criticism | LCGFT: Literary
    criticism
Classification: LCC PN3331 .M846 2025 (print) |
    LCC PN3331 (ebook) | DDC 809.3—dc23/eng/20250513
LC record available at https://lccn.loc.gov/2025019670
LC ebook record available at https://lccn.loc.gov/2025019671

Nello specchio ho visto che fra noi e noi stessi c′è un piccolo scarto, che è misurato esattamente dal tempo che mettiamo a riconoscere la nostra immagine. Da quel minusculo varco provengono, con tutta la psicologia, le nostre nevrosi e paure, i trionfi e cadute dell′io. Se ci fossimo riconosciuti instanta-neamente, se non ci fosse stato quel fugace intermezzo, noi saremmo come gli angeli, del tutto privi di psicologia. E non ci sarebbe il romanzo, che racconta—questo è la psicologia— il tempo che i personaggi impiegano a riconscere e a disconos-cere se stessi.

In the mirror I saw that between us and ourselves there is a small gap, a delay that can be measured exactly by the amount of time it takes us to recognize our own image. That minuscule opening gives rise, along with the whole of psychology, to all our neuroses and fears, all the triumphs and failures of the ego. Had we recognized ourselves immediately, had there not been that fleeting intermission, we would be like the angels, entirely devoid of psychology. And we would be bereft of the novel, which nar-rates—that is what psychology is—the time it takes characters to recognize and misrecognize, to avow and disavow, themselves.

GIORGIO AGAMBEN, *WHAT I SAW, HEARD, LEARNED*

Contents

Preface

The following book was created under the twin imperatives to remain short and to range far. Balancing these goals required decisions that shape both the structure of the argument and how this book can be read and utilized.

Although this is a book about the Western tradition of the modern novel, I have largely refrained from providing specific examples. For instance, I chose not to cite Marcel Proust's *Swann in Love* as an example of how we can experience jealousy, or Mohamed Mbougar Sarr's *La plus secrète mémoire des hommes* as an example of how we can experience postcolonial displacement. Beyond space constraints, this decision reflects the extreme disproportion between the vast corpus of novels and the singularity of individual experiences. How could one justify selecting Proust over Leo Tolstoy, or Sarr over Chimamanda Ngozi Adichie? As I argue throughout this book, novels themselves are singular, mutable experiences; they can only serve as examples on a taxonomic level (e.g., "X is an epistolary novel"), a framework outside the scope of this book. Moreover, I do not want to create the impression that following and evaluating the arguments in this book require prior familiarity with a large number of novels.

The problem of generalization extends to written reflections on reading experiences, which, for reasons I explain below, are hard to find. I include some of my own—they are, or try to be, as close to the occasion and the unfolding of my experience as possible, but precisely because they are mine and I am a professional reader, they tend toward the comparative, the general, the conceptual. I struggled, and am still struggling, with reaching the level of granularity these accounts should display. Writing and judging reading experiences are strange, somewhat elusive tasks. Originality, incisiveness, or similar qualities that we value in scholarly writing cannot serve as their criteria; in fact, such accounts may often carry a touch of the dullness we experience when listening to others telling us their dreams. Ultimately, such reflections are tentative precursors to the novelist's craft of narrating a character's experiences. They are, furthermore, inaccessible to the generative power of AI, which can assume identities and reproduce knowledge but never articulate the novelty experienced by a reading human body. In the final chapter I argue that despite their occasional awkwardness, articulated reading experiences are an important pedagogical tool for inviting readers into the novelty of reading experiences. The companion website, thenovelexperience.org, will collect and curate accounts of reading experiences and share prompts, classroom practices, syllabi, exercise sheets, and more.

Throughout the book I use the terms literature, narrative fiction, and novel interchangeably, but hope to clarify in the following pages why my focus is on works that are, in the broadest sense, fictional, require time to read, and are typically experienced alone. In its temporality, singularity, and exposure to fiction, reading is exemplary of the structure of human experience as this book unfolds it. That the novel became the dominant form of fictional narration in the West and that its realism implies the narration of a character's experience such that the reading mirrors what is being read are contingent historical developments. Some of the conditions of these developments are articulated in the chapters that follow.

To make the argument of the book more readable, I have opted to quote sources sparingly in the main text. Instead, each chapter concludes with short bibliographical essays that enable the reader to explore my sources and further their understanding if they chose to do so. Given the breadth of topics and authors discussed, my selection of sources is necessarily limited. A bibliography and additional resources are available at thenovelexperience.org.

The Novel Experience

Reading Experience I
Ralph Ellison, *Invisible Man*

In the summer of 2023, I began to read Ralph Ellison's 1952 novel *Invisible Man*. I must have read it decades ago but can't say I recalled much beyond a vague sense of recognition and difficulty. Now, in the wake of a wave of racist violence that had swept through my adopted country, I wanted to read it again. I had also come across, in preparation for the present project, Ellison's essays on the role of novels in American life, which led me to his writings on jazz. I remembered conversations with a friend involved in editing Ellison's papers and then, serendipitously, heard from another friend in Basel about an exhibition of Jeff Wall's "After *Invisible Man* by Ralph Ellison, the Prologue" that I had seen years ago at MoMa in New York City. A minute after deciding to reread it, a digital version was on my iPad.

Reading was slow, partly because medical treatments at the time left me tired and pensive. The language of the book itself resisted easy absorption, reminding me that American English is a foreign language—not only to me but also, as it were, to itself. As the narrator embarked on his adventures, the language seemed to splinter into dialects and speech patterns that, from Jim Trueblood to the brotherhood, shifted in tonal cadence and semantic rhythms. The same could be said of most "national" languages, including my so-called mother tongue; but in contrast to German, where linguistic diversity roots itself mostly in geography, American English seems more distinctly shaped by social, racial, and class segregations that traversed, and continue to traverse, the country. I remember trying to read Toni Morrison's *Beloved* when it had just come out, in my first year in the United States; although I was at the time teaching and writing in English, at decisive moments I could not understand what was being said in the novel.

Ellison must capture this diversity of speech—from the sermon on the "Blackness of Blackness" to the bloody oration after the battle royale to the hero's first experience of his own power of extemporaneous public speaking and its harnessing by the brotherhood—within the constraints of written language. I could sense how he chafes at the restrictions of alphabetic writing that make it so difficult to convey intonation, cadence, and bodily motion in written prose. I could sense this struggle, but only from afar, coming as I do from a language and culture that is notoriously scriptural. Nuance and tone in German is often indicated grammatically or by changes in the word order. The oral virtuosity of Black American languages in churches and song, though I can feel its persistence in jazz and hip-hop, belongs to an experience I cannot share. All I can do is acknowledge its presence and mourn its inaccessibility to me.

Six days into this reading, prompted perhaps by these reflections on the spoken, sung, and shouted word, I downloaded the audiobook. It is read by the actor Joe Morton—an imposing presence in each of his film and TV appearances—who delivers a masterpiece of recitation. It is hard to describe adequately the sensations his voice created in me: he is at the same time fearsome and authoritative, endlessly versatile but never exaggerated or comical. I know that members of the audiences of Charles Dickens's readings often broke down in tears or even fainted, and this feeling of being helplessly under the sway of a narrative becomes palpable in Morton's recording. His voicing of the diverse characters brings out the types of character encountered, and this gallery of types reconnected me to the experiences the narrator makes. The jealous and paranoid coworker, the maternal rescuer, the ideologue, the dropout, the fanatic—these are all characters I have encountered in my life, though not in this racial constellation.

Hearing and reading about slavery and racism in the United States evoke peculiar responses in German readers, expatriates or not: an intensified identification with the victims and an equally intensified revulsion against the perpetrators of injustice. I believe this stems from the historical fact that chattel slavery is the rare atrocity in which Germany was largely uninvolved, thus allowing German readers to reject any possibility of complicity. The blond man in Ellison's prologue cannot possibly have been one of us.

One of the hooks that pulls my reading of this novel forward is the portrayal of ideology, exhibited most glaringly by the members of the brotherhood. Political ideology (to be more specific, Marxism) is a different, more diffuse discursive force than racism, and disentangling the two preoccupies the hero until the end. Members of the brotherhood claim they cannot possibly be racist because their ideology forbids it. Racism for them is a matter of intellectual confusion and nothing else. Growing up in the 1970s in (West) Germany, the conflict between ideology and prejudice was the neuralgic center in the conflict between the generations. The country was still—and in many ways, still is— reverberating from a past when these two forces were inextricably linked; antisemitism was justified ideologically, and Nazi ideology had antisemitism as its vital center. One of the ways in which the younger generation tried to liberate themselves from that past was to espouse the opposite ideology—Marxism in its many gradations, ranging from mild social advocacy to Maoist zeal. I recall ideologues—they called themselves "cadres"—of the ilk portrayed in *Invisible Man* visiting high schools in the 1970s, trying to recruit students for their particular faction. There was something mysteriously alluring in the promise that the right ideology would erase murky sentiments like racism, antisemitism, and sexism. I sympathize with the narrator's temporary submission to ideology—to thought that is being thought elsewhere—because it promises to shelter him from the individual failures that seem to produce the inequities of racist experiences. In his journey, however, he experiences that ideological thought, abstracted from bodies and places, is empty thought. Yet what is supposed to replace it?

Is this attraction to ideology still comprehensible to younger readers? What takes the place of ideology today?

THESE ARE BUT A FRACTION of the sensations, thoughts, and ruminations that accompanied me while reading *Invisible Man*. They are not emotions but reflections and reactions, specific to this encounter at that time, between me and this book; in the way they came to me they seemed not to be mine but had me as their meeting point. They are singular and internal, but they record a real movement, a real change—on a most basic level I have become a (re-)reader of *Invisible Man*, part of a community formed and transformed by it.

My observations do not and cannot lay claim to originality; they do not attempt a new interpretation, or grapple with a new paradigm of analysis (a new "reading"). If I had been trained to attend to and articulate my reading experiences as I have learned to articulate impersonal judgments of literary knowledge, I am sure I could express them with more nuance and depth. Together, they make up the raw experience of my reading this book. I am an aged and professional reader; for young, "lay," Black readers, these reactions will be much closer to the unsettled core of their daily experiencing. For anyone, however, these experiences are the "real right thing" (Henry James's term) in our relation to literature.

And yet, should I venture to write about *Invisible Man* or to teach it in a lecture or seminar, none of these experiences would make it onto the page or on a slide. Neither in scholarly analysis nor in pedagogical practice and only rarely in nonacademic criticism does the reading experience come into sustained focus. In our conversations we may disagree on the interpretations of literary works, and on the choices of texts we read, but we cannot disagree that we have read them, and that this reading constitutes a temporally extended, spatially situated, and qualitatively specific, a singular experience. The "thatness" and singularity of reading experiences is the subject of this book.

Introduction

What has become of the experience of reading? Transformative as it can be, we have for it a sparse vocabulary and pay it little regard. In academic or para-academic settings, our reading always seems to take place in the past or in the future; the only temporality we are willing to admit is that we *have* read, or soon *will* (re-)read, *Invisible Man*. The rules of the language game "literary scholarship" do not readily accommodate a reader's reflections on the circumstances and vagaries of their reading, and these rules are often used to separate the objective judgments of the scholar from the subjective opinion of the critic or the connoisseur. What prompted my choice of this book over others? How long did it take me to read, what initial feelings did it elicit, how did these feelings change, how did the reading connect with other lived or read experiences? What reactions did the fictional characters, the length of the chapters, of the book, provoke in me? How do I communicate my reading experience to others, how do I account for it myself?

By brushing these and similar questions aside, we implicitly agree that reading isn't really an experience at all, but a disembodied, instantaneous mental absorption like "knowing," "understanding," or any other atemporal philosophical concept in which neither the object that is being understood nor the body that does the understanding has an essential role to play. In the pedagogy of literature, we actively discourage students from lingering on their reading experiences, guiding them instead to more "mature," abstract judgments.

Marginalized readers have always tried to break through the silence on experience; for them the discrepancy between their reading experience and the expectations of dispassionate scholarly assessment seemed too great to pass over quietly. W. E. B. Du Bois reading Johann Wolfgang von Goethe as a Black man, Leo Bersani reading Samuel Beckett as a gay man, Eve Kosofsky Sedgwick reading Henry James as a lesbian—they all disturbed the scholarly consensus that the experience of reading is not essentially linked to our reading of experience. Disruptive though their accounts were in the history of literary scholarship, the academic focus on knowledge soon turned these singular reading experiences into new scholarly paradigms or modes of "reading." This transformation of singularity into generality is the modus operandi of most academic disciplines, especially of those that, like literary studies, are asked to reflect on, or even justify, their place in the university of knowledge. In what follows, I will examine the history and philosophy of this transformation and offer a plea to give experience its proper space in the scholarship and pedagogy of literature.

There are several reasons why the reading experience has been marginalized in our engagement with literature. Most stem from two interconnected beliefs: first, that experiencing—compared to better defined activities such as judging, learning, or knowing—is too vague, too subjective, too tied to bodily presence to be effectively articulated and communicated. Second, that the primary aim of academic reading and writing about literature is not to deepen and enrich personal experience but to extract the knowledge it ostensibly contains. These beliefs, rooted in distinct theological and philosophical traditions, have deeply informed literary studies; disguising and forgetting them, and banishing the murkiness of experience in favor of knowledge and truth, were the price the modern research university demanded from literary studies for its admission to the scientific community.

This price, I will argue, was too steep and paid in the wrong currency: literary studies can never—and should never—

compete in delivering the most precise or valuable knowledge. Instead, its relevance within the university curriculum should rest on its unique ability to provide access to the irreducible singularity and depth of human experiences. This access is essential for the responsible acquisition and the social practice of knowledge. Placing the reading experience at the beginning of our reflection on literature and learning to accept the validity of these diverse experiences honor our actual encounter with literature and cultivate an invaluable skill: the ability to articulate, share, and shape our experiences, and to recognize this effort in others.

One defining feature of experience is its singularity. While we can, and should, strive to articulate and communicate our experiences, they remain our own and cannot literally be "shared." In every conversation about experience, therefore, we must recognize the uniqueness of another's experience and, just as critically, the incompleteness, the transitoriness, the fragility of our own. The invisibility of another's experience and the provisional nature of our own are brought into communication in the reading of literary works that narrate experiences—for example, in novels like *Invisible Man*. The reason why, I will argue (most insistently in chapter 5), that novels not only recount, but *are* experiences is to remind us that each is a singular work as well, and to show this without having to resort to the vocabulary of traditional aesthetics and narratology. Reading and discussing such works prepare us to encounter and appreciate, to experience singularity, as we accept the experience of a novel's protagonist, of a play's hero, of a poet's voice as singular and yet communicable.

In our eagerness to participate in the race for knowledge, we scholars, teachers, and lovers of literature missed the opportunity to host conversations about experiences. In colleges and universities, we frequently neglect to help undergraduates express their experiences, we fail to encourage graduate students to reflect on them, and we present ourselves, to students and colleagues, as having already read everything. We often dismiss the value of reading experiences shared in book clubs, blogs, or vlogs, and rarely incorporate in our research and teaching the rich tradition of literary reviews in newspapers and journals. With our focus on disembodied knowledge, we have maneuvered the study of literature into fragmented debates over critical positions while lamenting the precarious state of the field.

We have also deprived literary studies—especially the pedagogy of literature—of all defenses against the encroaching wave of AI tools capable of summarizing vast corpora and generating "critical" positions literally in the blink of an eye. The expansive conception of experience the following pages will unfold is contrary both to the notion of disembodied artificiality and to the privileging of intelligence in the approach to literature. AI may reason, even reflect, but it neither meditates nor experiences. On the positive side, probed and prompted in the right way AI may show us how to access and formulate our experiences as they lay buried under the weight of habit and judgment.

The marginalization of experience in literary studies stems largely from its portrayal as a flawed and unreliable way of engaging with the world. This perspective has deep roots in Western culture, reaching far back to ancient Greek metaphysics and its self-imposed mission to "save the phenomena": to give foundational reasons why the world is a well-ordered whole and not a chaotic tangle of events. Finite human experience was seen as inadequate for this mission, and the task delegated to the project of first philosophy—to the project of finding principles of explanation that precede, or transcend, experience. In the fusion of metaphysics and Christian theology, these principles were embodied in the omnipotent creator God. When at the dawn of Western modernity scholars and scientists—Galileo Galilei, René Descartes, and Joseph Justus Scaliger, to name a few from the sixteenth and seventeenth centuries—wanted to disentangle theology from the discourses of knowledge, it was again experience that was sacrificed, this time on the altar of a priori certainty and the demands of experimental measurability.

In my first chapter, I will briefly trace the logic and consequences of this sacrifice and show how the problem of experience persisted in the philosophies of Immanuel Kant and G. W. F. Hegel—systems of thought that still hold sway over contemporary theories of science, literature, and pedagogy. In their ambitious attempts to find philosophical foundations for the natural sciences, Kant and Hegel no longer excluded experience yet did not accept it as a self-standing source of insight either. Experience became tethered to conceptual classification and to the powers of judgment, retaining limited independence only in aesthetics and in religious dissent.

To reclaim the full scope of experience in general and the experience of reading literature in particular from these implicit restraints, we must look beyond the confines of Western traditions of thought. In the second chapter, I introduce the Buddhist philosopher Nāgārjuna, one of the most incisive thinkers of experience in the Eastern tradition. Writing and teaching in second-century Northern India, Nāgārjuna's *Root Verses of the Middle Way* (*Mūlamadhyamakakārikā*, hereafter as *MMK*) offers a perspective on experience unbound by the justificatory demands and ontological commitments of Western metaphysics. His radical, strikingly concise arguments are matched in the Western world only much later by two nineteenth-century philosophers, Friedrich Nietzsche and William James. Chapters three and four explore how these two unlikely contemporaries—unaware of Nāgārjuna and of each other—arrive at equally profound visions of the novelty and the purity of experience.

Fictional literature, particularly the novel, became a sanctuary for experience during the ice age of rational knowledge. In the fifth chapter, I show how the rise of the novel is linked to the survival and complexification of discourses of experience. Certain formal features of the novel—what I will later call its seriability—not only allow for the fictional record of unsanctioned experiences but also enable readers to enjoy reading as an experiential process. This interplay between the experiences in the text and the experiences we undergo in this reading reaches its zenith in the realistic novel of the nineteenth century. Here, the omniscient narrator presents experiences that, akin to those described by Nāgārjuna, Nietzsche, and James, defy division into subjects that have the experience and the events that constitute it.

The sixth chapter briefly examines the metaphysics of reading that for centuries has diminished the unbounded and novel experience of reading in favor of the need to decipher, to explain, to "lay out." Behind this need for explanation is the Christian dogma of divine revelation through the Bible such that salvation hinges on correctly understanding God's written word. These testamentary, recognitive, and salvational reading traditions leave no room for the private enjoyment or the singular experience of an individual reader. Even as contemporary literary theory shows the pitfalls of Christian and post-Christian hermeneutics, it often remains tethered to the project of extracting knowledge from fictional narratives.

In the seventh chapter I trace the outlines of a practice of reading novels experientially. Novels in the tradition of the West are almost universally concerned with fictional accounts of experiences. The reciprocal relationship between the experience of reading and the reading of experiences frees experience from the need to speak in the tongues of knowledge, allows it to find a language of its own.

The coda offers a few practical suggestions for guiding students and "lay readers" in the articulation of reading experiences and in the practice of accepting another's experience. It indicates that the encounter with Artificial Intelligence may help us to crystallize the quality of our experiences. It also extends an invitation to readers to contribute their own experiences—as readers and as teachers—to the collaborative platform thenov elexperience.org.

Bibliographical Essay

For the layers of impossibility in sharing anybody's experience, see Thomas Nagel, "What Is It Like to Be a Bat?," *The Philosophical Review*

83, no. 4 (1974): 435–450. For the history and importance of the exhortation to save the phenomena, see the classic account by Pierre Duhem, *To Save the Phenomena, an Essay on the Idea of Physical Theory from Plato to Galileo* (Chicago: University of Chicago Press, 1969). For a thorough discussion of singularity as a concept oblique to the "classical" concept of individuality, see Samuel Weber, *Singularity: Politics and Poetics* (Minneapolis: University of Minnesota Press, 2021), especially 13–31. As will become clearer in the following pages, I follow Weber in naming "singular" that which escapes the conceptual interplay of identity and diversity. Weber discusses the Western philosophical (and political) background of this singularity; I feel additionally justified by the Buddhist thought that the singular is empty of essence, that it has no core, no self that persists beyond its appearance. This use distinguishes it from the sociological use that seeks to understand the disaggregation of modern societies into singularities when it speaks (in Weber's and my usage nonsensically) of actors as "singular individuals"; see Andreas Reckwitz, *The Society of Singularities* (Cambridge: Polity, 2020).

Chapter 1 | Experience from Aristotle to Hegel

The way philosophical traditions evaluate experience marks the specific differences between philosophical systems in Western thought and the generic difference between Western thought and the philosophies of the East and Global South. The generality of this statement should be enough to deter any attempt at reconstructing, let alone intervening in, this history. Yet if this is a rich history, it is not a particularly contentious one, as it largely follows the shifting valuation of experience within broader intellectual developments and commitments in philosophy, theology, and the natural sciences. The starkest division lies between Western metaphysics and Eastern and Southern systems of thought, which evolved on vastly different timelines and only recognized each other as interlocutors after millennia. The following reconstruction leads up to the point where these asynchronous streams meet and offer a shared "radical" perspective on experience—announced in the *mūla* (Sanskrit: root) of Nāgārjuna's *MMK*, in Friedrich Nietzsche's late vision of an immanent, "eternal" world, and in William James's "Essays in Radical Empiricism."

The term "Western Metaphysics" gains specificity when understood as a system of thought that heeds the ancient imperative to "save the phenomena." From its roots in pre-Socratic wisdom and astronomy to its culmination in German and Anglo-American idealism, this task revolved around defining phenomena and ensuring their "salvation" through explication. The urgency of this mission originates in the practice of ancient astronomy, survey, and navigation, where identifying celestial bodies as recurring phenomena—as planets and moons—required the distinction between the moving celestial body—the ontic blob of matter—and its predicted path, its ontological horizon. To identify Mars as the planet Mars, astronomers had to identify it by its relative position to the fixed stars *and* they had to determine whether it followed its orbit, the path composed of innumerable previous observations. Without this identification, without the conjunction of the moving object and its path, the sky would be perceived as chaotic, full of unpredictable comets and useless for any calendric and navigational function.

This commitment to impose predictive order on observed phenomena—essential for the maritime and colonial success of ancient Greek *poleis*—rests on an implicit, unobservable assumption: that the world be a cosmos, an ordered structure rather than a chaos of unrelated events. A planet is a planet only when it reappears on its cosmic path, and it can do so only if we suppose that this path is part of an order that we can ascertain and predict. These cosmic suppositions are necessary; they are not derived from observation—rather, they make observation meaningful in the first place. There must be an order for any explanation to have a chance of success, and there must be a last principle upon which explanations can come to rest. We will encounter this "must" again in Immanuel Kant's transcendental deduction and will ask where this imperative originates.

As a consequence of supposing a cosmic order that grounds and sustains the cognition of any object or event, cognition turns into re-cognition. To explain, to understand something means to allocate it, to put it back, as it were, in its right place in the cosmos. Georg Wilhelm Friedrich Hegel's philosophy connects this mode of explanation to the question of theodicy and gives the most comprehensive account of this relationship between cognition and recognition.

As Jacques Derrida famously observed, any process of recognition must rely on technologies of retention and protention—

writing, first and foremost—that transcend the limitations of individual or generational experience. Ancient Greek colonial expansion and the ability to navigate beyond sight of land depended on star maps, instruments, and mechanical devices that replicated the motions of the heavens. Similarly, as both Hegel and Nietzsche realized, ancient Greek tragedy functioned as a cultural technology that dramatized the interplay of cognition as recognition both onstage (Oedipus) and among the audience.

Thus, "Western Metaphysics" can be understood as a collective name for those systems of thought aimed at elucidating the background assumptions that make the "again" in re-cognition plausible. Aristotle stripped the problem down to its barest elements and investigated it as the problem of locomotion, for him the most abstract form of change. In his *Physics*, he explored the tension between identity (of the moving body) and difference (of the path traversed); in books 7 and 8, he concluded that motion and change are meaningful concepts only against an unchanging backdrop. For the sublunar world, this constant is the rotary motion of the supralunar realm, where stillness (movement in place) and motion coincide. For the cosmos, it is the nous, the unmoved mover, who imparts motion without being himself moved. Since physics deals with "natural," terrestrial motion, and natural rotational motion does not exist on earth, metaphysics has to explain the stability of the cosmic order.

This genealogy of metaphysics, rooted in the problem of motion, has three important implications for the arguments that follow. First, it shows that the disregard for experience—particularly its novelty—is inherent in the salvational project of first philosophy, since its principles must transcend the limitation of human experience. Second, it opens the dialogue with Nāgārjuna, who, in the second chapter of the *MMK*, offers a trenchant critique of the distinctions between path, moving body, beginning, and end of motion, exposing the metaphysical assumption embedded in these concepts. Third, it highlights how the fusion of Greek and Christian metaphysics, wherein Aristotle's nous evolved into the creator God, resolved the inherent contradiction of an unmoved mover literally by fiat: by endowing God with unlimited creative power. This solution, however, raises a much more pressing question: Why, if God created it ex nihilo and therefore had unlimited options, is this world full of suffering?

Suffering is a human experience; Nāgārjuna goes so far as to say it *is* human experience. For the Greeks—as well as later for Nietzsche—it belonged to the tragic constitution of the cosmos. Christian apologists attributed suffering to humanity's desire for divine being—the snake had promised Eve that she would *be* like God. Her attempt cast humans into the hostility of God's world, into the frailty of their mortal bodies, into the instability and temporality of human experience. Experience, consequently, was disqualified not only as epistemologically unreliable but as tainted by sin. Throughout the history of Christianity, ardent believers tried to wash away this stain and claim direct experiences of God; the churches, Catholic and Protestant alike, did their utmost to invalidate and suppress these claims as presumptuous and heretical. Only in Eve's antitype Mary will the desire for God's being finally be fulfilled, initiated, as we will see, in a scene of reading.

It is worth noting here that Buddhism also begins with the "noble truth" that there is suffering, *dukkha*. However, this suffering—if "suffering" is even the right translation—is neither embedded in a cosmic structure nor punishment for a primordial fault. It arises, as we will see in greater detail, from the misunderstanding of phenomena as stable and substantive. Unlike the Christian narrative of mortal sin, this misunderstanding is remediable. In Buddhism, no phenomena require salvation, and no God need be justified in the process of relinquishing suffering.

The Scientific Revolutions of the sixteenth and seventeenth centuries necessitated a recalibration of the status of experience. On the one hand, scientists insisted that speculative, observational, and experimental insights must remain compatible with human experience—even those that contradicted immediate perception, such as the heliocentric universe with its stable sun and spinning earth. The target of this insistence was the popular belief in miracles and, in the scientific community, the lingering reliance on final causes. On the other hand, the laws of motion— to cite the culmination of this process of experimenting and reasoning in the work of Isaac Newton—could not themselves be directly experienced. Their claim to absolute certainty exceeded the finitude of human experience both in its intellectual and in its physical dimension. Kant repurposed the scholastic term "transcendental" for this new way of adjusting the finite capacities of human thought to the infinity of the homogenous universe.

One of the pivotal transformations ushered in by Newton's mechanics was the unification of the physical sciences. Newton not only demonstrated that geometry and mechanics were compatible discourses but also eliminated the qualitative difference between celestial and terrestrial motions. As an astronomer and especially as a theologian, Newton remained committed to saving the phenomena and justifying God and His creation. In the dispute between his delegate, Samuel Clarke, and his German antagonist, G. W. Leibniz, he refused to allow that the world could have all the resources of its being within itself; God had to be free to intervene in his creation at any time. This theistic reservation, so characteristic of Newton, faded rapidly in the fervent reception of his work, especially in France. The universality of Newton's laws inspired materialist thinkers to envision a self-sustaining world that required no further explanation and justification. In such a world, experience would simply be another process that follows laws and is animated by forces—attraction and repulsion—that can be quantified and compared.

David Hume drew different philosophical implications from Newton's mechanics when he speculated that human beings orient themselves in the world through relations akin to Newtonian attraction. He proposed that the mind passively experiences syntheses between ideas and impressions and that we are subject to these processes more than we "have" or even "make" them, as Kant later insisted. In his inquiries, Hume abandoned key tenets of earlier metaphysics: the givenness of the world and its need for justification, the identity and unity of the reasoning subject, and, most daringly, the central role of God in whom our ideas converge and who guarantees the cosmic order. In this constellation, experience rises above a priori reasoning and innate ideas; it is recognized, in all its temporality and incompleteness, as the sole foundation for making reasonable statements. Notably, Hume emphasized the social dimension of human experience, anticipating Hegel's argument about cognition as social recognition.

Yet in contrast to the optimistic visions of experience that we will encounter in Nāgārjuna, Nietzsche, and James, there is a sense of resignation and limitation in Hume's philosophy. This surely stems from its proximity to Newton's project, the overwhelming success of which relied on claims—notably on the universality of the laws of motion—that no empiricist philosophy could ever substantiate. Newton simply refused to speculate about the nature of his laws and of the forces they described; when pressed, he attributed them to the inscrutable power of God. This recourse was unavailable to the atheist Hume. Though he defended his views on empirical grounds, his concept of experience seems haunted by the absence of transcendental guarantees. His philosophy, for all its emphasis on experience, remains a dualism—one in which the invalidated realm of transcendental guarantees lingers like the "ghosts of departed quantities," to borrow the memorable phrase of his contemporary George Berkeley.

It is remarkable that Kant, reflecting on his encounter with Hume's empiricism, said it had "awoken" him from his dogmatic slumber—a choice of words that uses, quite literally, the language of Buddhism (Sanskrit: *budh*, "to awaken"). The notion of awakening to a truth, which also appears in Nietzsche, suggests that such insight is not the result of inference or derivation. While we can trace its proximate causes—in Kant's case: reading

Hume—the resulting thought emerges with a clarity and novelty that defies all deduction. In its suddenness and simplicity, awakening resembles the Christian experience of conversion, albeit with a key distinction: we awake *from* previous beliefs but convert *to* new ones.

Other aspects of Kant's project also align with Buddhist principles—unwittingly, since Buddhism played no role in his thinking. None is more important than the *Transcendental Dialectics*, which occupies the second half of the *Critique of Pure Reason* and discusses problems that frustrate any intellectual effort to solve them. Kant carefully shows why such questions cannot be decided and what the attempts to solve them reveal of those who try; the Buddha, listing fourteen questions nearly identical to Kant's, is much less patient and declares that he will remain silent when they come up. None of these questions—for example, does the world have a beginning? Is matter infinitely divisible?—can ever be answered with reference to human experience. Both thinkers share the same goal: to liberate individuals from fruitless speculation and instead equip them with the wisdom to navigate their world.

Despite these parallels, Kant's *Critique of Pure Reason* (1781; 2nd. (B ed.) 1787) avowedly remains a project committed to saving the phenomena. Unlike earlier efforts that remained focused on the phenomena of change and motion, however, Kant shifts his attention to the subjective conditions necessary for phenomena to appear to us at all. Newton asserted the absolute generality of his laws of motion; Hume exposed the epistemological limitations of human experience. Kant's critical inquiry seeks to answer a more fundamental question: How can human beings attain certainty about phenomena in the first place?

Kant's response turns on a novel definition of knowledge: we can know—know with the universality Newton demanded—only what we can actually or potentially experience. Although we may not encounter every instance of motion, we can, in principle, experience a body moving in time through space. By contrast, angels, being incorporeal and beyond spatiality, are outside the realm of possible human experience and, consequently, cannot become objects of knowledge.

There is, for Kant, no such thing as "pure" experience—an encounter with reality unmediated and unthought by the categories of the understanding. Knowledge arises from bringing the experience of phenomena "in" time and space "under" the categories with which we think. These categories—this is Kant's "overcoming" of Hume—are neither innate nor acquired through experience; they are transcendental: necessary preconditions that make experience and thought possible in the first place. The ancient astronomers, for example, could not have made their observations without transcendental assumptions about the homogeneity of space, the continuity of time, and the relation between cause and effect.

All of these assumptions converge in a proposition that stands at the apex of Kant's pyramid of cognition: "The 'I think' must be able to accompany all my representations for otherwise something would be represented in me that could not be thought at all, which is as much as to say that the representation would either be impossible or at least would be nothing for me" (B ed., 132). This endlessly parsed sentence gives us the most abstract formula for the conditions under which we can save—have firm knowledge of—phenomena: we must be continuously aware that the thought we are thinking is *our* thought and that it is our *thought*. Note that the formula with its strange "must"—whence would such an imperative originate if the proposition is the "highest point"?—still conserves the ancient injunction to save the phenomena. Like the ancient astronomers, Kant accepts something as given that already evinces an order (the universality of Newton's mechanics) and then reasons backwards toward the ultimate conditions that must obtain for this given to be possible.

Kant's system gives experience a necessary but undeniably subservient role. True, there is no usable knowledge outside of experience; but it is also true that, for Kant, experience itself cannot think. This ancient dichotomy between thinking and experiencing remains at the center of Kant's thought—even though he himself admitted that his thinking had been decisively shaped by the experience of being "awoken" by Hume's ideas. The motivation behind these constraints on experience is both noble and pragmatic: Kant sought to disqualify claims based on the supposed *truth* of subjective experience, whether they originated from religious fanatics asserting divine guidance or from the early Romantics who insisted on experiencing truth in love and nature. Though in later works, especially in his reflections on the role of aesthetics, Kant relented and accepted nature and the fine arts as ways of experiencing, and enjoying, the interplay of our mental faculties, even in this admission he maintained and reaffirmed the dualism of knowledge and experience.

Kant's radical framework had another far-reaching consequence: since the soul could never be an object of true knowledge, introspection as a means of articulating experiences lost its philosophical legitimacy. The long tradition of essayistic writing—where authors observed themselves and drew philosophical consequences—lost its standing as a valid method of knowing oneself. Introspection, once the hallmark of writers in the tradition of Michel de Montaigne, found a refuge in the domain of fictional representations. Meanwhile, the psychology practiced in Western research universities, shaped by Kant's definition of a priori knowledge, became largely quantitative and classificatory, focusing on reaction times, stimuli, and physiological measurements.

Nietzsche, deploring the sterility of clinical psychology, revived essayistic and introspective writing in German. Similarly, James defined his approach to psychology in opposition to the German tradition that he knew from his visits to Germany and from colleagues at Harvard.

Kant's idealist critics recognized and lamented the limitations he imposed and defended but were not prepared, unlike the early Romantics, to abandon the ideal of certainty in knowledge either. If it was the distinction between experience and conceptual thinking that produced all these limitations, they argued, then philosophy had to delve deeper. It needed to reach the foundation where thought and being—to us the maximalist language of thinkers like Friedrich Wilhelm Joseph Schelling and Hegel—had not yet diverged. This effort to deepen and broaden the scope of philosophy, provocatively titled *Wissenschaft* (science), transformed the question of certainty that had preoccupied both the individual sciences and Kant's epistemology into a grander task: determining and explaining an object's or an event's place in the knowable universe. Everything became a philosophical question: Why is the earth magnetic? Where does light come from? Is chemistry more advanced than mechanics? Posing these questions and identifying transitions from one domain of knowledge to the next meant that the harsh transcendental thresholds Kant had installed between concepts and experience could no longer persist; knowing meant searching for those moments on the continuum of knowability where human thought and natural phenomena intersected.

The concept that enabled these intersections and transitions between thought and nature emerged concurrently in philosophy, poetry, and in the natural sciences: *the organic*. Kant introduced it as a speculative tool in his late philosophy of art and nature; now it was turned against him. The organic became the mantra for overcoming the limits and limitations of Kant's ancien régime of philosophy and soon spread to all areas of intellectual and social life, uniting poetry, philosophy, and the nascent life sciences.

Schelling's combative *Darstellung meines Systems der Philosophie* (*Presentation of My System of Philosophy*) of 1801 is a prominent example of the many "systems" that were launched in rapid succession at the turn of the nineteenth century to kick away the Kantian ladder and redefine philosophy's foundations and ambitions. In this work, Schelling demonstrates how an idealist investigation can uncover in seemingly inert facts—in geological formations, chemical reactions, or Newtonian forces—the latent presence of "spirit," *Geist*, that would bloom into concepts, ideas, and, ultimately, into works of art.

An example of this approach is the idealist interpretation of light (*Licht*). Schelling invented a concept that would have a flamboyant career in the last quarter of the twentieth century, "Dekonstruktion," to describe how even the seeming identity of light is dependent on dark matter (which for Schelling, curiously, was iron). Light, in its constant struggle with its dark other, can serve as an organic intermediary between nature and spirit; it can be experienced and yet is utterly transcendent. The phonetic proximity of *Licht* and *Ich* (self) symbolized, for Schelling and his many followers, like Johann Wolfgang von Goethe, Johann Wilhelm Ritter, or Alexander von Humboldt, that the deconstructed, organic view of light could disprove Newton's hated mechanistic approach.

No account of the organic emergence of meaning—from stone to poem—proved more influential in Europe and the United States of the late nineteenth century than Hegel's *The Phenomenology of Spirit* (1807). Its original title, *The Science of the Experience of Consciousness*, conjoined the three terms that Kant had declared irreconcilable within a single philosophical framework. Hegel sought to reconfigure Kant's rigid distinction between experience and knowledge not as a static divide but as a dynamic narrative of progressive overcoming. He traced how human consciousness ascends from its most rudimentary claims to certainty—such as pointing to something and declaring, "this is this"—to a fully articulated understanding of its own operations and its embeddedness in a meaningful cosmos.

For Hegel, experience is the name for a process of testing, failing, and revising one's own presuppositions. It can become the subject of a science because in this process consciousness uncovers a logic—a logic in which the negation of what is initially present leads to the affirmation of this negation on a higher level of consciousness. For example, the inadequacy of pointing at an object as a means of achieving certainty becomes the impetus for reflecting on the modalities of perception itself. The contradictions and reversal consciousness encounters in the world are, in the final analysis, its own. The upward spiral of its path to self-consciousness and spirit is prescribed by this logic of recognition. Everywhere in the natural world, in history, art, religion, and society, this process of successively more "logical" recognitions takes place.

In Hegel's philosophy, then, experience is no longer dismissed as a lower, less sophisticated, "blind" faculty of human engagement with the world. Instead, it animates a logically evolving choreography in which human consciousness apprehends its objects, tests its concepts, and corrects its prejudices. *The Phenomenology of Spirit* shows how consciousness learns to recognize in objects the meaningful, "subjective" elements and thereby recognize itself. This recognitive form of knowledge as self-knowledge—the ability to discern meaning as already inherent in the phenomena we encounter—is the most comprehensive manifestation of the Western impulse to save the phenomena and to justify the world.

To the fullest extent possible, then, Hegel sought to provide explanations of what it means for human beings to have experiences. Rather than encasing it in a static system that declares it to be inferior to intellectual insight, he gives a dynamic account of experience that highlights its participation in all facets and phases of cognition. But in this explanation lie its limitations as well. What experience discovers has always already been there; its outward movement into the unknown, the *ex* of experience, is always inflected backward, "home," by the *re* of recognition. "Where are we really going? Always homeward," the early Romantic poet Novalis wrote. For all the progressive energy invested in uncovering the world, the same Romantic nostalgia wafts through Hegel's system.

The constraint at the other end of Hegel's explanation is his firm conviction that experience is something humans make rather than something that makes them. Even though he seems to recount the emergence of consciousness in the process of experience, it becomes clear—at the latest in the chapter on self-consciousness—that consciousness was there from the very beginning, waiting to be uncovered and activated. There never is a moment when experience is wholly untethered from the project of gaining conceptual clarity, never a moment of genuine novelty.

Hegel's philosophy was not only a triumph of idealist speculation; it also took firm roots in the social realities of the nineteenth and twentieth centuries. Pruned and flattened, it became the raison d'état of the Prussian state and its successors, shaping in particular its institutions of higher learning. The German research university, in turn, became a beacon for students worldwide and Germany's most successful intellectual export. The university determined what would be taught as science and what was considered *Bildung*, the intellectual and social lubricant that established new distinctions in a society that had ostensibly moved beyond the rigidity of inherited class divisions. The admiring biographies and commentaries that appeared on the 250th anniversary of Hegel's birth in Germany show that this tradition is alive and well at least in the country of his birth.

Hegel, of course, did not settle the debate about the status of experience, even if he liked to think so. As the nineteenth century drew to a close, the mental and physiological consequences of industrial capitalism made the call for the liberation of experience even more urgent. In Friedrich Nietzsche (1844–1900), we will encounter perhaps the most consequential of these voices in the German and European context. After Nietzsche's death, it is the catastrophe of the Great War that shatters a whole generation's access to their experience.

Interestingly, just as Kant's awakening to the problem of experience was triggered by his reading of Hume, so was Nietzsche's own awakening tied to his reading of Ralph Waldo Emerson (1803–1882), whom he discovered when he was only seventeen and who was the only writer whom he unreservedly admired throughout his life, including during the time when he wrote his *Zarathustra*. Emerson's writings, particularly the famous essay "Experience," became, in form and content, models for Nietzsche's thought.

Emerson, in turn, was a family friend of the James family, and William James (1842–1910) reminisced, wrote, and spoke

about him profusely and admiringly. No doubt his own thinking about experience, though it seems to arise from his empirical work in psychology, was deeply influenced by Emerson, thus
establishing an intellectual bridge to his German contemporary,
Nietzsche. Both thinkers, unaware of each other, developed a
radical and radically novel understanding of experience.

   To fully grasp the achievements of Nietzsche and James and
the ways in which they challenge core tenets of the Western tradition of thinking experience, it is instructive to step outside
that tradition. Thinkers like Martin Heidegger and Jacques Derrida promised such a departure, but remained entangled in the
tradition, expending most of their efforts on defining themselves
against it. Contrary to Derrida's assertion, there is an outside to
Western metaphysics and its conceptualization of experience.
Rationally formulated and argued, appearing contemporane-
ously with the sages in Asia Minor, mainland Greece, and Sic-
ily, Buddhism rejected the demands of religion and belief in
supranatural forces. Initially an oral tradition and only centuries later codified, it underwent its first reformation in the second and third century CE with the writings of Nāgārjuna.
Often seeming to argue directly against the presuppositions of
Western metaphysics, Nāgārjuna initiates and formulates the
thinking of what is commonly translated as the Middle Way.
This is the outside to which we now turn.

Bibliographical Essay

For an overview of Western philosophical approaches to experience, see
Martin Jay, *Songs of Experience: Modern American and European Varia-
tions on a Universal Theme* (Berkeley: University of California Press,
2005). Jay's valuable and extremely well-researched and structured account
is exclusively focused on Western philosophical concepts. Andrea Tagliapietra, *Esperienza: Filosofia e storia di un' idea* (Milano: Raffaello Cortina,
2017) is especially interesting when he discusses the ancient Greek antecedents of the modern problem of experience, as well as the relation of
experience to narrative, and he, too, ends with James, though he does not
discuss non-Western ideas of experience. Both Jay and Tagliapietra have
chapters on Walter Benjamin. For an analysis of Benjamin's position—

and of the role of experience in "revolutionary" philosophies in the shadow of the Great War—see Peter Fenves, "Pure Knowledge and the Continuity of Experience," in his book *The Messianic Reduction: Walter Benjamin and the Shape of Time* (Stanford, CA: Stanford University Press, 2011), 152–186. For the difference at the heart of every phenomenon between its "thatness" and its meaning, see Martin Heidegger, *Being and Time*, (Oxford: Blackwell 1985), 51–55. While they would appreciate his attention to the temporal unfolding of experience, none of the three thinkers we will engage with would regard Heidegger's famous question of the "meaning of being' as an original or necessary question.

For the transition from physics to metaphysics in Aristotle's *Physics*, see Walter Bröcker, *Aristoteles* (Frankfurt: Klostermann, 1987), 272–280. For the Leibniz-Clarke (Newton) correspondence, see Ezio Vailati, *Leibniz and Clarke: A Study of Their Correspondence* (Oxford: Oxford University Press, 1997), especially 165–192.

For a most "optimistic" interpretation of David Hume, see Gilles Deleuze, *Empiricism and Subjectivity* (New York: Columbia University Press, 2001). Deleuze emphasizes the role fiction plays in the constitution of subjectivity, much like Nāgārjuna, as we will see later. The phrase "ghosts of departed quantities" is from George Berkeley's assault on what he believed to be the trickery of infinitesimal calculus in *The Analyst* (1734), 18; https://www.maths.tcd.ie/pub/HistMath/People/Berkeley /Analyst/Analyst.pdf. For the emergence of mathematical certainty in physical science—the possibility of which Kant thought he had to demonstrate—see Alan Shapiro, "Experiment and Mathematics in Newton's Theory of Color," in *Newton: Texts, Backgrounds, Commentaries*, ed. I. B. Cohen and Richard Westfall (New York: Norton, 1995), 191–202. The progressive mathematization of physics coincides with the rise and ultimate supremacy of Newtonian science; see Peter Dear, "Mathematics Challenges Philosophy: Galileo, Kepler, and the Mathematical Practitioners" in his book *Revolutionizing the Sciences: European Knowledge and Its Ambitions, 1500–1700* (Princeton, NJ: Princeton University Press, 2009), 64–78.

Certainty has been the subject of some of the most celebrated works in the history of science, notably Alexandre Koyré, *From the Closed World to the Infinite Universe* (Baltimore: Johns Hopkins University Press, 1968) and Hans Blumenberg, *The Genesis of the Copernican World* (Cambridge: MIT Press, 1989). Philosophically, it formed the core of concerns for the development of Edmund Husserl's phenomenology in

The Crisis of European Sciences and Transcendental Philosophy (Evanston, IL: Northwestern University Press, 1970) and of John Dewey's pragmatism in *The Quest for Certainty* (New York: Minton, 1929). For Newton's theory and practice of experiments see Cohen and Westfall, *Newton*, 147–164. The great opponent of Newton's experiments was Goethe, who went so far as to liken Newton's "crucial" experiments (*experimentum crucis*) to the crucifixion of nature; see Joel Lande, "Acquaintance with Color: Prolegomena to a Study of Goethe's Theory of Color," *Goethe Yearbook* 23 (2016): 143–169.

For the similarities between Kant's Transcendental Dialectics and the Buddha's refusal to address unanswerable questions, see the translators' introduction to *Introduction to the Middle Way: Chandrakirti's* Madhyamakāvatāra *with Commentary by Ju Mipham* (Boulder, CO: Shambala Publications, 2004), 5–12. Kant's Transcendental Deduction and its "highest point" can be found in Immanuel Kant, *Critique of Pure Reason*, ed. and trans. Paul Guyer and Alan Wood (Cambridge: Cambridge University Press, 1998), 246 (B ed., 132) and 247n. A classic account of Kant's arguments for the transcendental anchoring of knowledge is given by Henry Allison, *Kant's Transcendental Idealism: An Interpretation and Defense* (New Haven, CT: Yale University Press, 1983), especially 81–114; and, on the other end of the spectrum, by Gilles Deleuze, *Kant's Critical Philosophy: The Doctrine of the Faculties* (Minneapolis: University of Minnesota Press, 1985).

Kant's aversion to psychological introspection is directed not against the tradition of Montaigne but against so-called rational psychologists who tried to demonstrate the immortality of the soul from concepts; see Gary Hatfield, "Empirical, Rational, and Transcendental Psychology: Psychology as Science and as Philosophy," in *The Cambridge Companion to Kant*, ed. Paul Guyer (Cambridge: Cambridge University Press, 1992), 200–227. Kant's popular and late writings are full of psychological wisdom and curious observations. His *The Conflict of the Faculties* (New York: Abaris, 1979) contains self-observations, for example "On Pathological Feelings That Come from Thinking at Unsuitable Times" (199), that would fit right into Tibetan meditation manuals.

For the transition from Kant to Johann Gottlieb Fichte to Schelling to Hegel, see Eckart Förster, *The Twenty-Five Years of Philosophy* (Cambridge, MA: Harvard University Press, 2017); for the rapid succession of antagonistic systems from the early 1790s to the 1820s, see Rolf Peter Horstmann, "The Early Philosophy of Fichte and Schelling," in *The*

Cambridge Companion to German Idealism, ed. Karl Ameriks (Cambridge: Cambridge University Press, 2000), 117–140. The editor's introduction to this volume (1–17) is extremely valuable. Schelling's surprising use of "Deconstruktion" is in Friedrich Wilhelm Joseph von Schelling, "Darstellung meines Systems der Philosophie," in *Schellings Werke*, ed. Manfred Schröter, vol. 3 (Munich: Beck, 1927), 66.

For Hegel's concept of experience, see Martin Heidegger, *Hegel's Concept of Experience* (London: HarperCollins, 1989). For an overview of Hegel's project, see Robert Pippin, *Hegel's Idealism: The Satisfaction of Self-Consciousness* (Cambridge: Cambridge University Press, 1989). For a lucid guide through the *Phenomenology*, see Terry Pinkard, *Hegel's Phenomenology of Spirit* (Oxford: Oxford University Press, 2023). For the importance of German universities in the United States, see Louis Menand, Paul Reitter, and Chad Wellmon, eds., *The Rise of the Research University: A Sourcebook* (Chicago: University of Chicago Press, 2017). A famous case study of the collective change of experience in the industrial age is Wolfgang Schivelbusch, *The Railway Journey: The Industrialization of Time and Space in the Nineteenth Century* (Berkeley: University of California Press, 2014). For Nietzsche's acquaintance with Emerson, see Benedetta Zavatta, *Individuality and Beyond: Nietzsche Reads Emerson* (Oxford: Oxford University Press, 2019), xiii–xx. The Sanskrit word for middle (and waist) is *mādhya*: the syllable *ma* indicates the elative (*ka* is the adjective ending); *mādhyamaka* thus means "middlemost," itself a typically self-effacing concept.

Chapter 2 | The Liberation of Experience

Nāgārjuna

B uddhism, whatever its doctrinal differences, is first and foremost a radical philosophy of experience. It begins with one individual's transformative experience, the awakening of Siddhārtha Gautama to the thought of dependent origination—an experience that, despite being shrouded in layers of Buddhist hagiography, is not more mysterious than Immanuel Kant's awakening to David Hume's arguments about experience or Friedrich Nietzsche's awakening to the thought of Eternal Recurrence. Gautama initially hesitated to codify his thought into doctrine, struggling to give it a form that would not compromise the amplitude of his experience. The earliest Buddhist texts are compilations of teachings attributed to him centuries after his enlightenment, shaped by the questions and interests of his interlocutors and acolytes. Like the Christian Gospels, these texts were collected and edited with the dual aim of consolidating the teachings and of divinizing their source.

When Buddhism first entered the philosophical conversations of the West—often presented as an amalgam of Buddhist and Hindu thought—it was branded as a philosophy of nothingness and quickly attracted the interest of those philosophers who were ready to abandon the project of metaphysics and its pursuit of salvation in first principles. In the nineteenth century, Arthur Schopenhauer, eager to reverse Georg Wilhelm Friedrich Hegel's dismissal of "Indian" thought, emerged as its most prominent advocate, presenting Buddhism as a pessimistic yet principled alternative to Western philosophy and religion. Nietzsche, inspired by Schopenhauer, envisioned Buddhism as the last and sweetest fruit of global nihilism and mused whether he himself might not become the "Buddha of Europe." Neither he nor Schopenhauer nor anyone else in the nineteenth century could fully grasp that Buddhism is not concerned with metaphysical or logical nothingness but with emptiness (*śūnya*) as an experience. Nāgārjuna's *Mūlamadhyamakakārikā*—the seminal treatise in which the systematic exploration of emptiness (*śunyavāda*) is for the first time on full display—became available in a reliable edition only beginning in 1903, too late for Nietzsche (and for William James) to recognize its resonance with their own ways of thinking.

As with other insights that later coalesced into religions or political doctrine, Buddhism underwent phases of sectarian conflict and doctrinal overgrowth. There are no extant writings from the time of Gautama's awakening in the fourth century BCE, and the Buddha himself would not have spoken the languages (Sanskrit and Pali) in which his teachings were first transcribed—a remarkable parallel to the emergence of Christianity, when Jesus's Aramaic teachings were translated into the Greek of the *koiné*. By the second century CE, doctrinal divisions among Buddhist schools threatened to obscure the experiential core of the Buddha's teachings. It was in this context that Nāgārjuna and the philosophy of the Middle Way emerged.

His "Radical (*mūla*) Verses (*kārikā*) of the Middle-Most Way (*madhyamaka*)" (*Mūlamadhyamakakārikā*, *MMK*) comprises twenty-seven chapters of concise, densely argued two-line verses. Written in Sanskrit, the text often engages with opponents' views through unmarked citation, making it challenging to discern when Nāgārjuna is speaking in his own voice. He argues logically, exposing infinite regress and contradictions in his adversaries' assumptions. Nowhere, not even in the dedicatory "prostration" before the Buddha, is there an exhortation to belief, or a reference to preternatural causes. A striking characteristic is his focus on dismantling assumptions rather than offering counterproposals of his own. When evaluating an opponent's proposition, he systematically examines every logical possibility—that it is so, that it is not so, that it is both so and not so, that it neither is so nor not so—and rejects them all, without offering a "truer" alternative. As we will see, Nāgārjuna regards the practice of making truth-apt statements as fatally flawed both from a logical and from a soteriological perspective.

The work begins with a dedication to the Buddha that makes use of the extreme density allowed by Sanskrit grammar; it invokes and characterizes what Nāgārjuna identifies as the Buddha's foundational insight, the axiom of "dependent arising" (*pratītyasamutpāda*). It states that every phenomenon, event, or situation exists only in dependence on something else. If everything has dependently arisen, then there are no substances that exist independently from others, no essences in which the actuality of an object would be grounded, no absolute beginnings, no first causes, no final ends, no identities, no subjects, no objects. Emptiness emerges as the absence of inherent determinations. Dependent arising and emptiness are two sides of the same thought.

The first chapter extrapolates the profound implications of this universal contingency: it transforms the notion of independent, causal origination—central to Greek first philosophy, Christian metaphysics, and certain Buddhist traditions—into the analysis of the infinite web of interdependent causes in which any event is embedded. There is no terminus to this network, no singular "efficient" cause initiating a series of events or creating another phenomenon anew. There is no efficient or creative cause outside imbuing the world with purpose: no Creator at the world's beginning, no Judge at its end.

This does not imply that reality is incoherent, or that it is simply a mirage. Borrowing from Western logical distinctions, we might say that Nāgārjuna converts the search for *sufficient* causes—causes *through which* something comes into existence—

into the investigation of *necessary* causes—causes *without which* something cannot exist. For instance, is a sprout's emergence as a sunflower caused by the sun, or by water, or by the soil, or perhaps by the gardener? Or does it not rather emerge from a network of all of these, and infinitely more, causes, and isn't the sprout itself the product of such causes? Differently framed: it is not the case that the novel *Creation Lake* was brought into existence by Rachel Kushner, but that without Rachel Kushner, and a whole host of other reasons, *Creation Lake* would not have come into existence. This is a decisive switch in perspective—it lowers the metaphysical stakes and makes the conditions of existence accessible to experience.

Through a tightly woven series of arguments, Nāgārjuna dismantles claims to first causes and independent existence. To assert such independence would entail attributing to entities a substantiality (*svabhāva*) that endures beyond their individuation in a particular intersection of conditions. Arguing for the identity and substantiality of objects or subjects over time requires, as we know from ancient Greek astronomers and from Aristotle, the antecedent distinction between the identity observed and the background (the path) against which it appears. Nāgārjuna counters that this distinction between identity and its other opens a relation of dependence and thus defeats its premise, the claim to firstness and substantial independence. The prediction of a path implies the priority of order before the things to be ordered. Every chapter of the *MMK* makes a version of this argument before finally turning it against its own premises.

The first chapter of the *MMK* is concerned with invalidating four pretenses of first causes, which led some interpreters to speculate that Nāgārjuna was in actual dialogue with Aristotelian metaphysics. The second chapter shifts its focus to motion, the very problem that compelled Aristotle to vault his physics with metaphysical speculation. In twenty-five stanzas, Nāgārjuna critiques the notion that motion can be distinguished in time and space from the moving body. What would ground such a distinction? What differentiates a path traversed (or yet to be traversed) by a body from any other segment of space? How could one conceive of motion that is not the motion of a particular moving body? How can we determine when motion begins, and when it ends? These questions, familiar to us from Zeno's paradoxes, from empiricist critiques, and from Henri Bergson's philosophy of motion, assume a distinctive trajectory in Nāgārjuna's treatise.

Nāgārjuna does not deny the reality of motion or argue that motion is always continuous. Instead, he contends that treating motion as existing independently of a moving body attributes to it an essence (*svabhāva*) persisting beyond its particular instantiation. Upon logical examination, this supposed essence reveals itself as dependent after all—motion cannot be conceived apart from a moving body, just as identifying a moving body depends on recognition, on internal or externalized memory. ("Is this the same celestial body we chronicled last year?") The same objection applies to other topics Nāgārjuna's opponents bring up: desire depends on its objects, perceptions on what is perceived, the self on its parts, fire on fuel, and so forth. Motion stands at the beginning of Nāgārjuna's treatise because it is, as Aristotle also argued, the most abstract form of change. If motion is regarded as codependently arising—as arising in dependence on the moving body just as much as the moving body depends on it—then it becomes an explicable occurrence. It is no longer an essence but a name for the momentary interdependence of body, space, and time. It is true that as this essenceless, empty phenomenon motion cannot be predicted with certainty; in the flux of conditions, it is always novel. Nāgārjuna is free to take the risk of proposing such an unpredictable and changeable world because he does not have to commit to a meaningful, predictable cosmos, or to a creator god whom it would embody.

Emptiness, as Nāgārjuna explicates it, has nothing in common with the nothingness and the nihilism Nietzsche suspected as lurking at the heart of Buddhism. Rather, it is the constant philosophical task to empty out, to void and avoid concepts, habits, institutions, and practices of their pretensions to essential validity. In their effort to explain change and uphold the idea of identity and order, the essentialists clutter the world with concepts and static entities, turning every phenomenon, every event into a first repetition and stifling the potential for true novelty. "All is possible when emptiness is possible. Nothing is possible when emptiness is impossible" (*MMK* 24, 14).

A less abstract example of Nāgārjuna's voiding of essences is his discussion of the Four Noble Truths, also in chapter 24. Surely, his imaginary opponent objects, you cannot deny that the Four Noble Truths that the Buddha himself proclaimed are essential to his message. To recall, these four truths are: there is suffering (*dukkha*), there is arising (of suffering through craving), there is cessation (of craving), there is a path (to the liberation from suffering). If these turn out not to be hard and fast truths, the rest of the doctrinal edifice of Buddhism itself is annihilated, including the "three jewels"—the infallible figure of the Buddha, his doctrine (*dharma*), and the community of adherents (*sangha*). Buddhism itself would turn out to be empty.

Yet that is exactly what Nāgārjuna argues. He shows that if the first truth, that suffering exists, were a pronouncement about the essence of the world (in the manner of Protestant ethics, say), it would condemn human existence to irredeemable misery, rendering all hopes for liberation—expressed in the third and fourth truths—misguided or futile. However, empirical suffering, analyzed from up close, really is disappointment with the transitory, conditioned nature of life. Suffering is not the valley of tears from which we need to escape and from which the monastic community needs to shield us, nor is it our helplessness in the face of tragic fate. It is the name we give to the insight that everything we encounter in our experience is "unstable" (*dustha*, badly standing), shifting, unreliable. What we experience, therefore, is of the same nature as we who claim to experience it—constantly changing, without firm identity, mortal, without any ground. Suffering in the popular sense of deprivation and pain arises only if we deny this emptiness of experience and grasp at essences and identities. As the experience of emptiness, suffering is morally neutral: just as we habitually complain about the transitoriness of all things, we could also learn to enjoy it as providing us with the spectacle of arising and disappearing that makes life exciting and beautiful. Nietzsche makes exactly this claim.

The craving for permanence in a world of dependent origination is the reason for suffering, not the cruelty of fate, as the Greeks thought, or original sin. By not embracing the fullness of our experience, we are the co-originators of our suffering—this is, after all, what the second truth confirms, which is as dependent on the first as the first is on the second. The third and fourth truths—that craving can be understood and thereby stilled, and that there is a nonmystical path to such stilling—are equally dependent on each other, and on all the others. There is, in sum, no truth so noble that it could refer to an independent essence. Rather than setting out a revealed doctrine, the Four Noble Truths destabilize and empty each other—but therein, in their emptiness, lies their transformative potential.

Nāgārjuna emphasizes again and again that suffering is not a passive stance toward an unjust world but the active experience of emptiness. As disquieting as the experience of constant change and transformation may be—especially if there is no framework to secure and predict outcomes—it alone harbors the possibility of radical novelty, of another experience. Nāgārjuna was well aware that this perspective is anything but reassuring: "By a misperception of emptiness a person of little intelligence is destroyed / Like a snake seized incorrectly, or like a spell incorrectly cast. // This is why the Buddha initially hesitated to teach this dharma / fearing that it would be impossible for the slow-witted to penetrate this dharma" (*MMK* 24, 11 and 12).

The strategy Nāgārjuna deploys throughout the *MMK* consists in emptying propositions and phenomena of their essence and showing that assuming atomic kernels of meaning and being would lead to contradictions or to the doubling of explanations (e.g., explaining motion through "motion"). He argues that the analysis of the contingent and fleeting conditions that intersect in a given event will give us a better view on our reality than conceptual speculation. Emptiness is not the Nothing of the Eleatic philosophers, not a counterproposal to traditional metaphysics and its claim to essences; it is, rather, an activity and an experience—the activity of first deconstructing and then avoiding proposed essences, and the experience of living without the solidity of ultimate reasons.

As we can see, Nāgārjuna's project aligns intriguingly with that of Kant's, as both propose the elimination of metaphysical claims that are not anchored in experience. However, where Nāgārjuna is willing to abandon the entire project of metaphysics and concentrate on empirical guidance, Kant, the defender of Newtonian a priori mechanics, clings to the idea of subjective identity as the bridge linking thought and its objects. For Nāgārjuna, as for most thinkers in the Buddhist tradition, the markers of human identity—such as perception, conceptual thinking, consciousness, and memory—exhaust themselves in their function; they co-arise with (are codependent on) their objects and would dissolve with them were it not for the desire, the thirst (*tanha*) for permanence that is at the core of suffering. Nāgārjuna's arguments against the notion of an enduring self carry—like Nietzsche's and James's—a concrete liberatory impetus: historical Buddhism sought to free the individual from the ineluctable strictures of the Indian caste system and its deterministic claims of natal identity and endless cycles of rebirth.

The disavowal of a self, even if it is as insubstantial a proposition as "the I think," leads to a consequence that Kant sought to avoid at all costs: that thoughts and experiences are not really "mine." In Kant's world, deeply concerned with establishing rules that separate normalcy from deviation, the idea of being visited by thoughts, dreams, or visions was a sign of possible madness; in Buddhist practice, letting thoughts come to one, attending to them, labeling them, becoming aware of their rising and falling away are, to the contrary, goals pursued with extreme effort. Later in life, Kant pondered whether being surprised by one's thought might indicate artistic genius. For us, it is a first indication that in Buddhism there is an opening for aesthetic practice, even if it is the aesthetics of experience.

Whenever it looks as though Nāgārjuna intervenes in traditional Western philosophical debates—as when he, like Hume, decomposes the self into "bundles" (*skandha*) of attachment, or when he, like Kant, reminds us that there are questions that human reason can never answer—we must remember that he pursued a different agenda, one in which the guidance of experience is the main path to liberation.

Among these differences there is, first, the insistence that emptiness—in contrast to logical negation, which can be theorized and integrated into a dialectical system—must engulf any theory that articulates it. If emptiness is the consequence of dependent origination, then a theory that argues against the assumption of independent essences is dependent on this assumption—and therefore itself empty. There cannot be an absolute emptiness persisting beyond the discovery of emptiness in the various topics in the *MMK*. Nāgārjuna, insisting on the centrality of the Buddha's awakening to dependent origination, concludes—to the dismay of Buddhist clerics—that the Buddha's teaching itself must be empty. "Blissful is the quieting of all grasping, of all conceptual proliferation / Never, and nowhere, has any doctrine (*dharma*) been taught by the Buddha" (*MMK* 25, 24).

Second, the notion of emptiness as experience dramatically impacts the amplitude of human existence. Like other thinkers in the Mahāyāna tradition, Nāgārjuna distinguishes between two truths, the truth of convention and the ultimate truth. This was partly a pedagogical device to bring laypeople into the community of followers without burdening them with the full doctrinal weight of Buddhist philosophy. More profoundly, however, it is a recognition that the world of essences may be empty but still has efficacious reality. It may be ultimately true that we are not possessed of an essential identity that stays with us for all our lives, but the conventional ways in which we organize our communities, define our laws, and interact with each other rely on identity and individual responsibility. The Western notion of ideology tries to capture the same insight, though it still clings to the notion that there is a ground against which ideology reveals itself as "false" consciousness.

The axiom of emptiness, by contrast, in criticizing and invalidating the essences propagated by the world of conventions, invalidates its own status as "ultimate" truth: it is itself codependent on its object of criticism—convention—and therefore empty. The truth of the world of conventions—in the language of Buddhism, samsara—is simply that it is, against its own declarations and knowledge, the result of conventions, and therefore empty. The world of ultimate truths, nirvana, cannot be an alternate world in which all the distortions of the conventional world are rectified, for this would essentialize this alternate world and make it subject to the same criticism as that levied against the conventional world. The only way to conceive of the relation between the two truths is to say that the ultimate truth is the conventional world experienced *as* conventional. Nirvana (the ultimate truth) is not paradise or heaven—it is this world in which we live but experienced as the world of convention. "Whatever is the limit of *nirvāna*, that is the limit of *samsāra* / between the two, not the slightest difference can be found" (*MMK* 25, 20).

Experience, in the fullest sense it acquires in the Madhyamaka worldview, thus entails maintaining a parallax view on the world. It means questioning those experiences that have sedimented into conventional knowledge, judgments, and habits; it means giving space to the novelty of unforeseen intersections and networks of conditions; it means attending to one's own experiences as ever provisional and changing. But it also means accepting, seeing the reality of conventional institutions and interactions and taking seriously their dynamics and consequences. The Middle Way Nāgārjuna envisages is not a path on which we seek out the comfortable middle, the compromise between two worldviews, but the constant undoing of one by the other: of the conventional world by realizing that its essences are fictions, of the ultimate world by realizing that it depends on the conventional world for its truth. Emptiness, after all, is always emptiness of something.

To sustain this parallax view might seem too difficult or too onerous a task, especially for us laypeople engaged in the complexities of daily life. Yet in more limited contexts, we already practice this balance. One example is the experience of raising young children. Their world is full of fantastic essences that we as parents must take seriously while gently steering them toward emptying their world of monsters, imaginary friends, hostile elements, and desperate attachments to objects. It will not do to insist on the emptiness of their worlds when they are not yet able to make such distinctions themselves, and when they see us—as they invariably will—accepting conventions and essences in our own world.

The example that is important for the present context is our experience of fiction. The relationship between conventional and ultimate truth mirrors the ways readers engage with prose fiction in Western cultures since the end of the eighteenth century. Before that time, elaborate devices of concealment—such as the invention of a fictitious editor—signaled a text's fictional status while preserving its meaningfulness. Since then, however, through a complex network of codependent developments— which are the subjects of later chapters—we have come to accept modern novels as works of fiction that we appreciate by simultaneously suspending and acknowledging their fictionality.

When reading a novel (or watching a film or TV series), we do not typically focus on the mechanisms by which it constructs its semblance of reality. Instead, we accept the story that is being told (or shown) as a coherent account of relations between events and characters even as we remain aware of, enjoy even, its dependence on the multiple conditions that brought it before our eyes and ears. We accept, in Nāgārjuna's terms, the characters and events in a novel as essences while being fully aware that they are empty. Reading novels allows us to experience that conventional truth is not falsehood masquerading as truth, but truth in the form of convention. It is for this reason that reading novels relates to living our lives.

If it seems preposterous to claim that the experience of modern novels is linked to Nāgārjuna's Middle Way, in the following I will marshal the help of his modern avatars, Nietzsche and James, to make exactly this point.

Bibliographical Essay

For the history of Buddhism, see Donald S. Lopez Jr., *The Story of Buddhism: A Concise Guide to Its History and Teachings* (New York: Harper-Collins, 2009). For the centrality of experience to Buddhism—so central that there isn't a special term that would differentiate it from other faculties—see John Holder, ed., *Early Buddhist Discourses* (Indianapolis: Hackett, 2006), xii–xiii; the book also gives a good impression of how these early discourses "sounded," and how different, in comparison, the *MMK* are. For the Western misunderstanding of Buddhism as a philosophy of Nothing and Nihilism, see Roger-Pol Droit, *The Cult of Nothingness: The Philosophers and the Buddha* (Chapel Hill: University of North Carolina Press, 2003). For a decluttering of the Buddha's biography see Bernard Faure, *Les mille et une vies du Bouddha* (Paris: Seuil, 2018).

For my understanding of the *MMK*, I have consulted three editions/commentaries:

1. Mark Siderits and Shōryū Katsura, *Nāgārjuna's Middle Way: Mūlamadhyamakakārikā* (Boston: Wisdom Publications, 2013), which gives a transliteration of the Sanskrit original, an English translation, as well as a commentary. (The translation is not undisputed; see Claus Oetke's review of the book in *Acta Orientalia* 76 [2015]: 190–243.)

2. Jay Garfield, *The Fundamental Wisdom of the Middle Way* (Oxford: Oxford University Press, 1995); Garfield translates from the Tibetan text and provides important continuous commentary. Garfield may be the most influential interpreter of Nāgārjuna in the United States and has a significant YouTube presence. Where I quote directly from the *MMK*, I use Garfield's translation, followed by chapter and verse numbers. Two of his essays are particularly important: "Dependent Arising and the Emptiness of Emptiness: Why Did Nāgārjuna Start with Causation?," *Philosophy East and West* 44, no. 2 (1994): 219–250, and, with Graham Priest, "Mountains Are Just Mountains," in *Pointing at the Moon: Buddhism, Logic, Analytic Philosophy*, ed. Mario D'Amato, Jay L.

Garfield, and Tom J. F. Tillemans (Oxford: Oxford University Press, 2009), 1–82.

3. Emanuela Magno, *Nāgārjuna: Logica, dialettica e soteriologia* (Milano: Mimesis, 2012). Magno, who includes a transliteration and Italian translation, is interested in Nāgārjuna's relation to the history of Western logic, and in the soteriological consequences of the emptiness of emptiness. One of her main interlocutors is Guy Bugault, whose immensely interesting *L'Inde pense-t-elle?* (Paris: PUF, 1994) gives an overview of the main currents of Indian philosophy and their reception in the West before concentrating on the *MMK*. Magno and Bugault set Nāgārjuna's logic against the background of Western, more precisely Aristotelian, logic and its rules and exclusions.

None of them goes as far, however, as Lutz Geldsetzer, who in *Nāgārjuna: Die Lehre von der Mitte* (Hamburg: Meiner, 2010) translates Nāgārjuna into German from a fifth-century CE Chinese translation, and claims that Nāgārjuna (most obviously in *MMK* 1.1) is responding directly to Aristotle's theory of the four *aitiai*. Appealing though this line of interpretation might be—Geldsetzer basically argues that Nāgārjuna abolishes three of the Aristotelian causes but keeps the *causa formalis*, which would align it with the aesthetic reading I am proposing—it has come under withering criticism by Claus Oetke in his review of the book in *Orientalistische Literaturzeitung* 107 (2012): 304–309. An interesting comparative study of Aristotle and Nāgārjuna could begin with the relation of the four causes to the Four Noble Truths and follow their different paths from that intersection.

Two books by Jan Westerhoff were very helpful for my understanding of Nāgārjuna: a monograph on the *MMK* (*Nāgārjuna's Madhyamaka: A Philosophical Introduction* [Oxford: Oxford University Press, 2009]) and a broader overview (*The Golden Age of Indian Buddhist Philosophy* [Oxford: Oxford University Press, 2023]). For an in-depth analysis and translation of Nāgārjuna's chapter on motion, see Dan Arnold, "The Deceptive Simplicity of Nāgārjuna's Arguments against Motion: Another Look at *Mūlamadhyamakakārikā* Chapter 2," *Journal of Indian Philosophy* 40 (2012): 553–591.

For Nāgārjuna's use of the fourfold rejection (*catuskoti*), see David Seyfort Ruegg, "The Uses of the Four Positions of the Catuskoti and the Problem of the Description of Reality in Mahāyāna Buddhism" in his *The Buddhist Philosophy of the Middle: Essays on Indian and Tibetan Madhyamaka* (Somerville, MA: Wisdom Publications, 2010), 37–112.

For readers wanting to both get a chapter-by-chapter commentary on the *MMK* and a taste of fifteenth-century Tibetan thinking about the middle way, there is RJE Tsong Khapa, *Ocean of Reasoning: A Great Commentary on Nāgārjuna's "Mūlamadhyamakakārā,"* trans. Geshe Ngawang Samten and Jay Garfield (Oxford: Oxford University Press, 2006).

On the question of "giving reason"—a transformation of the problem of theodicy, itself a transformation of the problem of "saving the phenomena"—and the principle of sufficient reasons in Western metaphysics, Martin Heidegger's lecture and seminar (*The Principle of Reason* [Bloomington: Indiana University Press, 1996]) is remarkably clear. For the continuing importance of this principle even for Hegel's idealism, see Pirmin Stekeler, *Hegels Phänomenologie des Geistes: Ein dialogischer Kommentar* (Hamburg: Meiner, 2014), 69–71. There is naturally a great deal of divergence about how to understand emptiness. Surely it is not a negation that annihilates its position, nor is it a Hegelian *Aufhebung*, where the negated is somehow conserved and carried over to a higher level—the arguments in the *MMK* are always the same, even if they are differently formulated. Apart from Ruegg's and Magno's discussions mentioned above, an interesting vein to follow is to look at the genealogy of the "number" zero, which arises in Indian mathematics at about the same time as Nāgārjuna's *śūnya* and has the same name. This provenance excited the interest of Western semioticians (Julia Kristeva, *Semeiōtikē: Recherche pour une sémanalyse* [Paris: Seuil, 1969], 273–275) and soon that of historians of culture, both analog (Brian Rotman, *Signifying Nothing: The Semiotics of Zero* [Stanford, CA: Stanford University Press, 1987]) and digital (Jussi Parikka, *What Is Media Archeology?* [Hoboken, NJ: Wiley, 2012]). More likely is the provenance of *śūnya* from the speculation of ancient grammarians; see David Seyfort Ruegg, "Mathematical and Linguistic Models in Indian Thought: The Case of Zero and *Śūnyatā*," in *The Buddhist Philosophy of the Middle*, 1–12, and Claudio Bertocci, "Lo Zero," in *Zerologia: Sullo zero, il vuoto e il nulla*, ed. Claudio Bertocci, Piero Martin, and Andrea Tagliapietra (Bologna: il Mulino, 2016), 10–34.

There is considerable debate in the critical literature whether chapters 26 (on the twelve links that constitute dependent origination) and 27 (on wrong views) are later interpolations, given that chapter 25 ends with the cumulative statement that the Buddha—true to the self-unsettling dynamism of dependent origination as emptiness—has never taught any doctrine; see Bernhard Weber-Brosamer and Dieter M. Back,

Die Philosophie der Leere (Wiesbaden: Harrassowitz, 2005), 100–102. It is interesting to consider whether these last chapters were not inserted to rein in the revolutionary and dogmatically disturbing consequences of Nāgārjuna's thought. In Buddhism, doctrine often manifests as numbered lists—four truths, eightfold path, three jewels, twelve links, etc.—and domesticating dependent origination in such a list may just have been a way of defusing the antidogmatic thrust of Nāgārjuna's verses. Significantly, when the guardian of Buddhist doctrine, the Dalai Lama, teaches the *MMK*, he begins not with the dedication or with chapter 1 but with chapter 26; see Barry Kerzin, *Nāgārjuna's Wisdom: A Practitioner's Guide to the Middle Way* (Somerville, MA: Wisdom Publications, 2019), 1–4.

For the topic of fiction and fictionalism in relation to Buddhism, see Charles Crittenden, "Everyday Reality as Fiction—A Madhyamika Interpretation," *Journal of Indian Philosophy* 9, no. 4 (1981): 323–333; Mario d'Amato, "Buddhist Fictionalism," *Sophia* 52, no. 3 (2013); and Tom Tillemans, "How Far Can a Mādhyamika Buddhist Reform Conventional Truth? Dismal Relativism, Fictionalism, Easy-Easy-Truth, and the Alternatives," in *Moonshadows: Conventional Truth in Buddhist Philosophy*, ed. the Cowherds (Oxford: Oxford University Press, 2011), 151–166.

Reading Experience II
Sylvia Townsend Warner,
The Corner That Held Them

For a brief period in the second half of 2020, Twitter was heaven for me. I had curated my feed to include only family, friends, and people whose literary opinions and taste I valued. Guided by their advice, I spent the summer reading novels written by American women authors, such as Paula Fox, Christina Stead, Jean Stafford, and Elizabeth Hardwick. Eventually, I came across the English writer Sylvia Townsend Warner's novel *The Corner That Held Them* (1948; hereafter *TCTHT*). I read it on an iPad, which has a lot of obvious advantages but lacks the tactile sense of a book's length—of knowing how far one has gone and of feeling sad or impatient about its impending end. Initially, this loss of physical format was annoying, but it soon contributed to the blissful disorientation I experienced as I read.

My bliss and enchantment deepened as I recognized the novel's liberal but peculiar use of the "reality effect," where attention to seemingly unimportant detail is inserted to tighten the warp and weft of story and plot. I became fascinated by these pockets of poetic knowledge despite my general skepticism toward historical novels. Warner luxuriates in depictions of medieval practices, objects, and characters, but not in ways that serve the advancement of the story. Indeed, if a story requires a beginning, a middle, and an end, then *TCTHT* has no story. Set in an English nunnery, the narrative begins in the time of the plague in 1349 and progresses, sometimes in very short, sometimes in longer intervals, until 1382 (the dates are the chapter titles). There are recurring characters but no protagonists; there are many subplots but no overarching plot; there is an ending, but it does not tie events together. Warner recounts innumerable conditions that lead to an event but steps back from drawing causal connections.

This open frame is the setting in which the details can sparkle. I quickly came to trust Warner's superior knowledge of medieval culture—a little research shows that she was an accomplished medievalist—because unlike in historical novels, I do not sense the heavy toil of research, nor the nudge toward allegorical, presentist interpretation. Even such a devastating event as the Black Death is reduced to yet another difficulty the nuns must deal with. After a while, I relax my vigilance and read on as if there is no message or moral behind this chronicle; history is just what happens, experienced by the nuns as it happens; in the instances where they themselves attribute ulterior meaning to an event—interpreting the failure of a building structure as divine punishment, for example—it turns out to be wrong or insignificant.

The solidity of fact paired with the aimlessness of the plot at first triggered all my interpretive alarms. Am I missing something? Reading Warner's Wikipedia page I discover, and then read, her openly lesbian novel *Summer Will Show*—also a work of historical imagination, but very much plot driven and defined by desire. Yet in *TCTHT*, the absence of sexual desire as a narrative agent—the absence of narrated sexual desire, not of sex— is at first bewildering, then soothing. The nuns are ambitious, mad, eccentric, and each is rendered in vivid but narratively insignificant detail, as are the manor, the servants, the landscape, the plague. Attributing overarching meaning to the setting and characters of the novel—apart from sexual desire I tried religious blindness, feminism in the church, and exoticism of the Middle Ages—feels forced and diminishing.

This novel lets us participate in "the varieties of religious experiences," and Warner goes to great lengths to bring them before us in their full "thatness" and authenticity—there is no other desire that she exposes as the "truth" behind the nun's experiences. The moment one were to read religiosity as a cover for "realer" realities or truer desires, the reading experience would change and revert to the scrutiny of critical reading practices. I begin thinking what I would do with a book like this in the classroom before I catch myself and remember that aptness for the classroom is not a meaningful attribute for any novel. Some novels can only be recommended.

The overall sensation that grips and delights me is the release into the pure movement of reading—being pulled forward by the unfolding of the story, being stopped midnarrative by an extravagant description, by an unusual adjective, by an elaborate simile. I put the book down, read a passage again, or just marvel at it. The slightly oppressive feeling I get when reading, for example, Gustave Flaubert's *Madame Bovary*, where we must suspect every element of description to be in the service of the plot, and vice versa, evaporates. It is as if the genre "novel" has come apart at the seams and released the lyricism of language from its servitude to narration. Long though it is—about 400 pages—I don't want it to end, and it seems the author didn't either.

Chapter 3 | The Genealogy of Experience

Nietzsche

Friedrich Nietzsche's scandalous first book, *The Birth of Tragedy* (1871), was many things: an outburst against the narrow-mindedness of classical philology, a celebration of archaic over classical art forms, and a tribute to Richard Wagner's vision of the total artwork. At its core, though, it was a forceful reclamation of aesthetic *experience* over historical and philological analysis. However speculatively, Nietzsche recounts every step in the emergence of Greek tragedy from the perspective of the spectator, for whom the representation of tragedy becomes the tragedy of representation: the tragedy of being separated from the vision on the stage, from the hero who is being sacrificed, from the gods who demand the sacrifice, and from the community who witnesses it. In pointed rejection of Georg Wilhelm Friedrich Hegel's absorption of tragedy into the ineluctable progress of Spirit—the tragic sacrifice of Antigone, for Hegel, signals the emergence of rational civic laws—Nietzsche highlights the cruelty, the repetitiveness, the irrationality of tragic representation and, at the same time, celebrates the abandonment with which the spectators embrace it. This *Rausch*—the inebriation that arises from losing oneself in another experience—is Nietzsche's early aesthetic and speculative version of the "pure experience" that William James discovered in his laboratory around the same time.

The book is also a first subterranean engagement with Buddhist visions of experience, though the deepest connection, that between the Eternal Recurrence of the Same and Nāgārjuna's axiom of Dependent Arising, appeared ten years later. What Nietzsche in *The Birth of Tragedy* calls the wisdom of Silenus—"Wretched, ephemeral race, children of chance and tribulation, why do you force me to tell you the very thing which it would be most profitable for you not to hear? The very best thing is utterly beyond your reach: not to have been born, not to be, to be nothing. However, the second best thing for you is: to die soon"—invokes the mainstream Buddhist argument that the origin of *dukkha* (suffering) is "having been born" into a world of transitoriness. In this early phase, Nietzsche's sympathy for Buddhism is still very much beholden to Arthur Schopenhauer's view that Greek tragedy and Buddhism both despaired over the pain of individuation. We already know that Nāgārjuna makes short shrift of this stance: for him, at the heart of human suffering is ignorance—in particular the ignorance of believing that something can be the sole cause of something else or, more fundamentally, that anything *is*, unconditionally. Suffering, he says, is another name for the search for first, last, or sole causes.

Nietzsche's invocation of tragedy at this stage targeted the blind progressivism into which Hegel's philosophy of history had morphed in the second half of the nineteenth century. Tragedy, Nietzsche insisted, could not be overcome and "elevated" in the experience of consciousness but had to be experienced repeatedly and ritually to rouse a polis from complacency. The opposition he opens between the Apollonian arts of convention and the Dionysian vision of the groundlessness and meaninglessness of existence resembles the Buddha's insight in the two truths, except that it remains confined to an annual festival and subservient to the needs of the polis and its metaphysics.

There is an air of bravado about this early work, meant to counter the pessimistic and paralyzing consequences Schopenhauer drew from his insights into the crushing futility of existence. Nietzsche celebrated the defiance of tragic heroes who do not accept suffering quietly or withdraw into the passive contemplation of art. Tragic repetition, for Nietzsche's heroes as well as for the spectators, is not the repetition of an identical event but, since every tragedy was "new" and part of a citywide competition, the return of a difference that reaffirms the rebellion against the gods and the fate that hangs over them. The tragic hero is the first to say to the gods: "Was *that* life? Well then! One More Time!"

By reintroducing the repetitiveness and absolutism of tragedy into his vision of classical antiquity, Nietzsche also wanted to suspend the metaphysical question of justification and salvation of the world, a constant concern of this pastor's son. He delighted in showing that pre-Socratic philosophies and cultures had no interest in this question, and that the operatic interpretation of tragedy—by Wagner, for example—transformed the task of saving the world into an aesthetic attitude: "Only as an aesthetic phenomenon is existence and the world eternally justified." To the tragic hero's bravado, he added the defiant irresponsibility of the modern artist who observes the spectacle of the world from beyond the confines of morality and teleology.

Nietzsche's youthful attempt to synthesize ancient tragedy, Wagnerian opera, and Schopenhauer's proto-Buddhist worldview famously failed, not least because he recoiled from Wagner's eagerness to bring the German Reich into this triangle. Following his break with Wagner, Nietzsche pointedly turned to France—the "hereditary enemy" (*Erbfeind*) recently defeated and humiliated by the Second Reich—and immersed himself in the writings of French moralists and essayists from the sixteenth to the eighteenth centuries. These mostly aristocratic writers had developed, through observation, introspection, and bemused thought experiments, a rich vocabulary of psychological and cultural criticism. They restored for him access to a world and a sensibility that academic psychology, in the wake of Immanuel Kant's verdict against psychology, had closed and barricaded with its quantitative methods.

Nietzsche admired the French writers as "free spirits," unbounded by systematic, political, or moral constraints. Intellectual heirs of Michel de Montaigne, they were irrepressibly curious, let their attention wander, and expanded the limits of articulating experience. Importantly, they developed specific literary forms to reflect the logical playfulness and intermittent temporality of experiential thinking: the essay and the aphorism. So captivated was Nietzsche by these agile and experimental writings that he would never write an academic "book" again.

With this shift in style, Nietzsche also abandoned the notion that truth results from concentrated conceptual labor or from expansive historical description. Aphorisms are the diametrical opposite of the style required in German academic *Wissenschaft*. They each have their own rhythm, their own cut and polish, their own perspective, often voicing alternative viewpoints and experiences without explicitly marking or judging them. This porosity of Nietzsche's writing to others' experience became a hallmark not only of his published works but also of his extensive notebooks. Some of these notebooks were published after his death without regard for the polyphony of voices they contain, essentializing concepts in a manner wholly incompatible with the thrust of Nietzsche's late philosophy.

The most calamitous consequence of the editorial flattening of his thought—aside from the well-known falsifications that turned his writings into bellicose, antisemitic propaganda—was the misunderstanding of Nietzsche's core vocabulary. Just as Nāgārjuna's *śūnya* (emptiness) was misunderstood as a nihilistic doctrine and thereby turned from an instrument of critique into its opposite, an essence, Nietzsche's Will to Power was quickly essentialized as a category in which he supposedly formulated his ultimate explanation of the world—his version of explaining, and thereby saving, the phenomena. Though the book with this title was later discovered to be a tendentious compilation, even such influential readers as Martin Heidegger and Gilles Deleuze regarded these three words as a single fundamental concept.

William James observed that "philosophy has always turned on grammatical particles," such as prepositions and conjunctions. They underscore that philosophical concepts are relations, not isolated modules that require a frame in which they find their place. So it is with Nietzsche's key terms. Will-to-Power, importantly, is neither will nor power; it is the will's wanting of and striving for power, and power's solicitation of the will. The distortions that Nietzsche's genealogical approach seeks to bring to light are often the result of mistaking a mutual relation for a single essence. Less systematically but also more expansively and attentively than Nāgārjuna, he goes through a series of phenomena that look like independent essences—compassion, morality, duty, God, religion, knowledge, mastery, slavery, art, the body—and shows them to derive from an effort to stabilize, to overpower, the radical contingency of a world that is no longer in the hands of God.

The Death-of-God—the loss of the path in which we expect an object to move, the collapse of any framework in which phenomena can be stabilized—is in turn codependent on the Will-to-Power. As aphorism 125 of Nietzsche's *The Gay Science* so dramatically narrates, "we," in search for power, have murdered God and now must perpetually fill this void with our own manifestations of power. Yet just as the will is dependent on power and power on the will, so is the Death-of-God internally a codependent relation: that between radical finitude (death) and radical infinity (God). When the Christian God, tripped up by his own insatiable Will-to-Power, imposed his will on the world by creating it ex nihilo, paradoxically and inevitably this imposition of omnipotence brought the *nihil*, the Nothing into the world as well. It manifests externally as the time before creation and imposed the linearity of beginning and end on the world— Nietzsche reclaims this excluded time in the eternity of recurrence; internally, in the created world the Nothing appears as death. Following Nāgārjuna, we can say that the radicality and subsequent death of the Christian God emptied emptiness of its experiential core.

The problem of the Death-of-God, then, extends beyond secular erosion of Christian values to the impossibility for the omnipotent God to die and to experience the anguish that so thoroughly shapes the lives of his creatures. That is why, for Nietzsche, Dionysus is the counterfigure to the Christian God: Dionysus, patron of tragedy, knows what it is like to die. Nietzsche's deep compassion for Jesus stems from his recognition that the Son of God had to die, if not for the sins, then for the hubris of the Father. In heresies like Arianism and Gnosticism, where the belief in the trinity and in the death of God as Son had weakened, God appears as trapped in the same predicament as every absolute ruler: he is dependent on power. In Nietzsche's genealogical analysis, God is dead because he cannot die, which is tantamount to saying that he cannot make experiences. In the terms this essay explicates later, this also means that God cannot read.

Mobilizing these internally and externally codependent terms, observing and tracking their interplay in history and their traces in psyches collective and individual, is the work of genealogy. In contrast to positivistic history, the suffocating effects of which Nietzsche had analyzed in his early writings, genealogy provides a means of identifying and following the concepts and practices that seek to stabilize and ground the flux of phenomena. Analytically, the genealogist does the same work Nāgārjuna had done in his dispute with the clerics who essentialized the dharma; but Nietzsche in addition reconstructs how the solidification of conventions played out in the history of Western Europe. He recognizes the emptiness in the conventions of the West, and the desperate attempts to fill it with ever more abstract values. Even after its historical demise, Christianity survives as nihilism, as the Nothing that attracts and harnesses the will and prevents its striking out for new experiences.

A third prepositional term co-arises with the Death-of-God and the Will-to-Power: the Eternal-Recurrence-of-the-Same. Nietzsche gives his awakening to this thought a time and place, and his alter ego Zarathustra staggers and groans under its near-unbearable weight. In *The Gay Science* and in *Thus Spoke*

Zarathustra, he stages elaborate scenarios to evoke the experiential gravity of this insight. Nietzsche thus insists that Eternal Recurrence is not simply a logical thought or a concept but a profound experience—an experience so all-encompassing that it changes the ways we inhabit the world. Like all experiences, it can be approached from the perspective of the experiencer or from that of the experienced; it can be understood as a thought experiment designed to challenge our ethical choices or as a cosmological theory about time, space, force, and matter. Nietzsche and his interpreters have attempted to "prove" Eternal Recurrence from both angles, as an ethical postulate or as a cosmological theory. Ultimately, though, experiences cannot be proven.

This is not to suggest that Nietzsche's encounter with the thought of the Eternal Recurrence is a mystical event. It is an awakening to a rational path out of the dilemmas of Western metaphysics and its drive to save the phenomena. By taking temporality seriously—distinguishing eternity from infinite spatial division into before and after and breaking the linear conception of time that had shaped the world since the demiurgic myths of Hesiod, Plato, and the Hebrew bible—Nietzsche seeks to return things to the freedom of being the codependent same they have eternally been: to the freedom of no longer being split between the idea and its avatar, between the passive and active side of representation, between being a wandering blob of matter and a planet following its orbital path. In dismantling ideas of origination, purpose, and redemption, Nietzsche thrusts the world back into the groundlessness and boundlessness, the *a-peiron*, from which philosophers since the pre-Socratics had endeavored to rescue it. Zarathustra's apotheosis of the Earth, his hymnic invocation of the sun and the stars, are his attempt to welcome the Same back from the exile of representation.

In a well-known interlude in the *Twilight of the Idols*, "How the 'True World' Finally Became a Fable," Nietzsche recounts the history of Western metaphysics as a six-step sequence of the "error" that is the division between the true and the conventional world and that, in the last two steps, clearly reminiscent of his own awakening to the consequences of the Eternal Return, is finally undone:

5. The "true world"—an idea that is of no further use, not even as an obligation—now an obsolete superfluous idea, *consequently* a refuted idea: let's get rid of it! (Bright day; breakfast; return of *bon sens* and cheerfulness; Plato blushes in shame, the pandemonium of all free spirits.)
6. The true world is gone: which world is left? The illusory one, perhaps? . . . But no! we got rid of the illusory world along with the true one! (Noon; moment of shortest shadow; end of longest error; high point of humanity; INCIPIT ZARATHUSTRA.)

A world without a double, one in which the scintillating surface is not obscured by the darkness of a metaphysical backdrop, "the seductive flash of gold on the belly of the snake Life"—this was Nietzsche's most profound experience. It was the insight he believed he was the first to make and that burdened and exhilarated him in equal measure. His later works, particularly *Ecce Homo* and *The Antichrist*, overflow with gratitude for a world that, freed from its imaginary double, sparkles with the surprise of novelty. The Same that recurs is not the numerically identical—it is not the same old, *das Selbe*—but rather the constellation of innumerable conditions that might bring forth the same kind of event. Everything that occurs and recurs is simultaneously familiar and novel, including the self. The marvelous phrase at the beginning of *Ecce Homo*—"and thus I recount my life to myself"—captures this interplay between familiarity and novelty.

Entrance into this world of genuine experience is reserved for those who relinquish the Will-to-Power in its most insidious form: the Will-to-Knowing. Twice in his *Zarathustra*, Nietzsche uses a phrase that astonishes even in a book brimming with metaphorical flourishes. In the chapter "On Redemption," he exhorts the will to give up its futile resistance to the intangibility of the past: "All 'it was' is a fragment, a riddle, a grisly accident—until the creating will says to it: 'But I will it thus! I shall will it thus!' But has it ever spoken thus? And when will this happen? Is the will already unharnessed from its own folly?" Similarly, in the chapter "On the Sublime Ones," ostensibly directed at the "heroes" of knowledge and science, he observes: "To stand with muscles relaxed and with an unharnessed will: this is most difficult for all you." Unharnessing one's will—dropping the yoke—(Sanskrit: *yoga*), laying down one's burden—these are phrases older than Nietzsche might have imagined.

Indeed, the Eternal Recurrence of the Same as the path to genuine experience is—and must be—the return of a very old worldview: Nāgārjuna marshaled similar arguments against the believers in motion behind the moving body, in time that is not present, in fire without fuel, or in a self that transcends a singular human existence. Ultimately, the Eternal-Recurrence-of-the-Same and the axiom of dependent origination (*pratītyasamutpāda*) articulate the same view of the world, with the important distinction that Nietzsche's vision had to pass through the crucible of Platonic and Christian beliefs in creation, causation, and purpose.

Whether an event—an *Augenblick* in Nietzsche's Goethe-inspired lexicon—is conceived as the result of infinitely many antecedents and consequences or as shaped by an infinite web of conditions: both perspectives converge on the fundamental insight that we must learn to live in a world without beginning and end, without purpose, without ground.

Only in such a world is true experience possible. Only when all barriers are removed—whether they take the form of nostalgia crystallized in moral prejudice, desire and thirst for stability (*tanha*), Will-to-Power reified in religion and dogma, or resentment dictating political decisions—only then can experience unfold as the experience of the infinite:

> *In the horizon of the infinite.*—We have forsaken the land and gone to sea! We have destroyed the bridge behind

us—more so, we have demolished the land behind us!
Now, little ship, look out! Beside you is the ocean; it is
true, it does not always roar, and at times it lies there like
silk and gold and dreams of goodness. But there will be
hours when you realize that it is infinite and there is
nothing more awesome than infinity. Oh, the poor bird
that has felt free and now strikes against the walls of his
cage! Woe, when homesickness for the land overcomes you,
as if there had been more *freedom* there—and there is no
more "land"!

Nietzsche's furious attack against atrophied, disembodied
forms of knowing, against harnessing cognition to what is already there, completes his life-long crusade against what we now
can recognize as an aspect of artificial intelligence—the view
that to know is to read, reassemble, and rearrange the fragments
of the past, to subject them to the ordering prompts of a reader
who wants to fill a void rather than launch into an uncertain
future. His training as a classical philologist had acquainted him
with modes of scholarship that are essentially large language
models; opposing their nostalgia with the parallax view of genealogy became his life's mission. Other ways of reading are possible, he insisted: a philology of the future that in every moment
participates in the novelty of experience.

While Nietzsche's relationship to Nāgārjuna is subterranean,
unacknowledged, and rooted in the shared rejection of any
ground uniting their worlds, his relationship to two nineteenth-
century thinkers of experience, Charles Darwin and Ralph
Waldo Emerson, is more overt and tangible. Nietzsche could not
fail to notice that Darwin, too, had shattered the compressed
timeline that had framed the natural world into epochs far too
brief to allow for any explanation other than divine intervention
or mechanistic causality for the origin and fixity of species. In the
language of Nietzsche, the anti-Platonist, and Nāgārjuna, the
reader of the Heart Sutra, the central issue was the status of
forms. Darwin agreed that forms are empty—formal similarities

between members of a species result not from intrinsic essences but from external conditions and contingent interactions.

Nietzsche saw his idea of a basic Will-to-Power in all beings validated by Darwin's accounts of survival, in particular his insistence that "will" must not be misconstrued as conscious intention, nor "power" as its end. Nietzsche must have been struck by Darwin's recognition that the dynamic interplay between selection and adaptation is best understood as an experience that nature herself makes, one where it is never preordained which is the active, "subjective" side and which is the side of "objective" resistance. Evolution is not a bildungsroman in which the organism first seeks to overcome, and then adapts to, environmental constraints; rather, the organism *is* the manifestation of these constraints as much as it extends and reshapes them. This co-origination of subject and object, figure and ground, becomes the narrative principle that Nietzsche employs in his genealogies and archaeologies of morals, religions, emotions, and institutions. It also anticipates the psychological analyses of absolute experiences that we will encounter in James's work.

Emerson was a lodestar for Nietzsche like no other author. From his earliest schoolboy writings to the epoch of *Zarathustra* and beyond, (the German translations of) Emerson's essays provided Nietzsche with a model for thinking and writing about experience. They also offered him a way to experience writing in a more supple format than the, at times, ponderous *Essais* of Montaigne. Emerson—admirer of Goethe and his concept of "tender empiricism"—approached experience not as a faculty in opposition to intellect but as a genuine source of insight. For Emerson, experience develops as it proceeds, incorporates reflection, and conceives of the experiencing self as something perpetually strange and remarkable to itself. Nietzsche adopted Emerson's critique of compassion and philanthropy, understood "representative men" as exemplars of a new aristocracy, and deeply felt the sense of tragedy and finitude that pervades Emerson's life and writing.

Darwin and Emerson—the latter in very concrete ways—were lodestars also for James. In James's late philosophy, we see an attempt to construct a microphysics of experience, a project that unwittingly would connect Nāgārjuna's and Nietzsche's thought to the realities of the industrial world.

Bibliographical Essay

For a convincing reading of the experiential dimensions of The Birth of Tragedy, see David Wellbery, "Form und Funktion der Tragödie nach Nietzsche," in Tragödie–Trauerspiel–Spektakel, ed. Bettine Menke and Christoph Menke (Berlin: Theater der Zeit, 2007), 199–212; a shorter version of this essay was published as "Nietzsche on Tragedy" in Michael Kelly, ed., Encyclopedia of Aesthetics (Oxford: Oxford University Press, 2024). For the contradictory experience of tragedy and its importance for the entirety of Nietzsche's oeuvre, see Jim Porter, The Invention of Dionysus: An Essay on "The Birth of Tragedy" (Stanford, CA: Stanford University Press, 2000). For a first orientation in the vast literature on Nietzsche and Buddhism, see Robert G. Morrison, Nietzsche and Buddhism: A Study in Nihilism and Ironic Affinities (Oxford: Oxford University Press, 1999); Freny Mistry, Nietzsche and Buddhism: Prolegomenon to a Comparative Study (Berlin: de Gruyter, 1987); and Antoine Panaïoti, Nietzsche and Buddhist Philosophy (Cambridge: Cambridge University Press, 2013), 17–87.

I have not found a sustained and mutually informed cross-reading of Nietzsche and Nāgārjuna. Nietzsche's dictum "I could be the Buddha of Europe—but that would be the opposite of the Indian one" appears in Friedrich Nietzsche, *Nachgelassene Fragmente 1882–1884* (Berlin: de Gruyter, 1988), 109. The wisdom of Silenus quotation is from Friedrich Nietzsche, "The Birth of Tragedy," in *The Birth of Tragedy and Other Writings*, ed. Raymond Geuss and Ronald Speirs (Cambridge: Cambridge University Press, 1999), 1–116, 23. The reference to birth as the cause of *dukkha* can be found, for example, in Bikkhu Bodhi, ed., *Noble Truths, Noble Path: The Heart Essence of the Buddha's Original Teachings* (Somerville, MA: Wisdom Publications, 2023), 104.

The question of aesthetic cosmodicy is discussed in Raymond Geuss's introduction to his and Ronald Speirs's edition of *The Birth of Tragedy*, xxii–xxvi. For Nietzsche's turn to the French moralists, see Robert Pippin, *Nietzsche, Psychology, and First Philosophy* (Chicago: University of

Chicago Press, 2011). Their common ancestor, in turn, was Michel de
Montaigne, one of Nietzsche's favorite writers. For a philosophy of the
aphorism, see Andrew Hui, *A Theory of the Aphorism* (Princeton, NJ:
Princeton University Press, 2019), 151–176. The cultural history of Nietzsche's "rescue" first from the falsifications of the Nietzsche Archive in
Weimar and then from the suspicion of GDR administrators has just
been told by Philip Felsch, *How Nietzsche Came In from the Cold* (Hobo-
ken, NJ: Wiley, 2024).

In his famous Nietzsche lectures, Martin Heidegger argued at length
that Will to Power is a metaphysical concept, an essence with which
Nietzsche demonstrates his belonging to the very tradition he seeks to
abolish. That the Will to Power as essence is, for Heidegger, the order
(*der Befehl*) illuminates in a flash the background—the (ridiculously self-
contradictory) Nazi slogan "Führer befiehl, wir folgen!" (Leader, order, we
follow!)—against which his increasingly uncharitable readings of Nietzsche are set: Nietzsche must be aligned with fascism so that Heidegger's
criticism of him can serve as a (post-factum) distancing from his own
early enthusiasm for the Third Reich. Heidegger himself was on the
board of the Nietzsche Archive and had proposed a plan for the reedition
of the notes contained in *Der Wille zur Macht*; see Marion Heinz, "Edition und Interpretation: Zu Heideggers Auseinandersetzung mit Nietzsches *Wille zur Macht*," *Nietzsche-Forschung* 30, no. 1 (2023): 3–19; and
Sebastian Kaufmann, "Der Wille zur Macht, die ewige Wiederkehr des
Gleichen und das Sein des Seienden: Heideggers 'Aus-einander-
setzung' mit Nietzsche," *Nietzsche-Studien* 47, no. 1 (2018): 272–313.
Heinrich Meier (in "Nietzsches Wille zur Macht und die Selbsterkenntnis
des Philosophen," *Nietzscheforschung* 30, no. 1 [2023]: 127–139) has argued
that Will to Power is a critical concept that Nietzsche uses to uncover
the errancy of the will, rather than celebrate it.

William James's remark about the importance of grammatical particles in philosophy can be found in his "A World of Pure Experience"
in *Writings, 1902–1910* (New York: Library of America 1987), 1161. The
master of philosophizing with prepositions is, of course, the Heidegger
of *Sein und Zeit* (Tübingen: Niemeyer 1986): "being-in," "being-with,"
"being-towards," "being-there". . . . The inability of God to die without
losing his divinity—in contrast to Nietzsche's Dionysus who affirms his
own destruction—is the interpretive matrix with which Hans Blumenberg has analyzed the emergence of modernity; for the most concentrated
version of this argument, see his *St. Matthew Passion*, trans. Helmut

Müller-Sievers and Paul Fleming (Ithaca, NY: Cornell University Press, 2022). Nietzsche's dating of the thought of the Eternal Recurrence of the Same appears most prominently in his *Ecce Homo* (*The Anti-Christ, Ecce Homo, Twilight of the Idols, and Other Writings*, ed. Aaron Ridley and Judith Norman [Cambridge: Cambridge University Press, 2005], 123), but the fact that thoughts can come to one because they are not the same as their thinker is fundamental to his late philosophy. See, for example, his *Beyond Good and Evil: Prelude to a Philosophy of the Future*, ed. Rolf Peter Horstmann and Judith Norman (Cambridge: Cambridge University Press, 2002), 17: "Thought comes when 'it' wants, not when 'I' want."

Martin Heidegger, in his first and more charitable reading of the Eternal Return, remarks expansively on the experiential nature of this thought; see his *Nietzsche: Erster Band* (Stuttgart: Neske 1998), 229–246. The phrase "unharnessing the will" occurs in Nietzsche's *Thus Spoke Zarathustra*, ed. Adrian Del Caro and Robert Pippin (Cambridge: Cambridge University Press, 2006), 112 ("On Redemption") and 92 ("On the Sublime Ones"). That Nietzsche cannot mean numerically identical lives recur eternally has been shown repeatedly, for example by Paul Loeb, "What Does Nietzsche Mean by 'the Same' in His Theory of Eternal Recurrence," *The Journal of Nietzsche Studies* 53, no. 1 (2022): 1–33; and Gerard Visser, "Der unendlich kleine Augenblick," *Nietzsche-Studien* 27, no. 1 (1998): 82–106. "How The 'True World' Finally Became a Fable" is in Nietzsche, *The Anti-Christ, Ecce Homo, Twilight of the Idols, and Other Writings*, 171. The infinite horizon aphorism is in Friedrich Nietzsche, *The Gay Science*, ed. Bernard Williams (Cambridge: Cambridge University Press, 2001), 119. The aphorism following is the famous madman story in which the death of God is announced. Section 109—the one with the repeated exhortation "Hüten wir uns!" ("Let us be vigilant!")—is Nietzsche's attempt to describe a world in which nothing has to be saved, in which everything recurs to the state of finally being the same. "Philology of the Future" (*Zukunftsphilologie*) was the sneering title of Ulrich von Wilamowitz-Moellendorff's review of Nietzsche's *Birth of Tragedy* (Berlin: Borntraeger 1872); for a positive reading of this notion, see James I. Porter, *Nietzsche and the Philology of the Future* (Stanford, CA: Stanford University Press 2002).

For Nietzsche's reading of Darwin, see Morrison, *Nietzsche and Buddhism*, 73–87. For Nietzsche's intensive reading of Emerson, see Dieter Thomä, "Jeder ist sich selbst der Fernste: Zum Zusammenhang zwischen

Personaler Identität und Moral bei Nietzsche und Emerson," *Nietzsche Studien* 36, no. 1 (2008): 316–343; Mason Golden, "Emerson Exemplar: Friedrich Nietzsche's Emerson Marginalia: Introduction," *The Journal of Nietzsche Studies* 44, no. 3 (2013): 398–408; Mason Golden, "Emerson-Exemplar (Autumn 1881) (KSA 9:13 [1–22] and KSA 9:17 [1–39]): Translation and Excerpts," *The Journal of Nietzsche Studies* 44, no. 3 (2013): 409–431; and Bendetta Zavatta, *Individuality and Beyond. Nietzsche Reads Emerson* (Oxford: Oxford University Press, 2021).

Chapter 4 | **The Microphysics of Experience**

William James

It is tempting to pair William James's works with Friedrich Nietzsche's—*The Varieties of Religious Experience* with *The Antichrist* and *The Genealogy of Morals*, *The Principles of Psychology* with *Human, All-Too-Human* and *Daybreak*, and the *Essays in Radical Empiricism* with *The Gay Science* and the more discursive portions of *Thus Spoke Zarathustra*. Both men were convinced that experience had to be freed from its subservience to knowledge and convention, both saw in Ralph Waldo Emerson an example of what such freedom could look like, and both gleefully disregarded philosophy's injunction against introspection, experiment, and experience. Yet James, though he certainly knew the tragic dimensions of life, was of a more serene philosophical temperament than Nietzsche. Unlike the solitary wanderer at 6,000 feet, he was intimately familiar with the actual variety of others' experience: his large family, his extended travels, the patients he observed in his lab at Harvard, the reading, talking, and lecturing he did to understand religious experiences in their vast diversity, his abiding interest in what we now call paranormal phenomena—they furnished James with data and insights that allowed him to grasp the singularity, the subtlety, and finally the absoluteness of experience.

A continuous line connects James's early empirical work in clinical psychology to his late essays in radical empiricism, and this line runs parallel to Nāgārjuna's and Nietzsche's thought. Despite his seemingly conciliatory and at times garrulous tone, his late essays propose the most far-reaching rethinking of experience prior to such philosophical iconoclasts as Georges Bataille and Gilles Deleuze.

James's *Psychology: Briefer Course* (1892), the condensed revision of his seminal *Principles of Psychology* of 1890, though structured as a textbook, dismantles the static view of separate faculties, of distinct states of mind that correspond to distinct external events. The taxonomic impulse of Immanuel Kant, already weakened by the organicism of Georg Wilhelm Friedrich Hegel and his followers, dissolves here into a dynamic, interactive, and concrete analysis grounded in observation, empirical data, and scholarly synthesis. At this stage in his career, James did not position his *Psychology* as an alternative to idealist philosophical investigations, of which he was well aware. The opening sentence of the famous chapter on "The Stream of Consciousness"—"The order of our study must be analytic"—is not so much a challenge to philosophy as an exhortation to eliminate speculative and deductive reasoning that has slipped into the discipline undeclared. In his later writings, however, he extracted from his textbook those insights that would destabilize core tenets of Western philosophy, in particular the "unity of consciousness" and the view that experience is something this consciousness "has."

An early indication for James's break with the philosophical tradition is his concept of "fringing." Since René Descartes and John Locke, philosophers have posited as irreducible units the distinct "idea" and the distinct consciousness that thinks them. Under these presuppositions, the most pressing concern has been to account for the relation between consciousness and ideas, specifically the relation called knowing with its attributes of certainty and clarity. Drawing on introspection and clinical observations, James refutes the assumption of atomic ideas and isolated consciousnesses, and the need for their transcendental deduction. Every idea, he counters, has around it a halo, or fringe, of relations that connects it to other ideas; every thinker is traversed by streams of thoughts that intermingle, transform, and bleed into one another. Traditional philosophical and psychological investigations arbitrarily segment this stream and then associate that segment with a single consciousness that has them and with a single event that it represents. They also impose transtemporal identity to both thought and thinker even though no thought ever recurs in the same way twice to a thinker immersed in her temporal and social "stream." In James's view, classical philosophy of consciousness, in its pursuit of scientific certainty, first created artificial isolates that then require elaborate ("transcendental") arguments to connect them.

James opposes to this self-imposed conundrum an account in which every aspect of our relation to the world remains resolutely empirical, including—and this may be his boldest step—the relations between our ideas or, to use Kant's terminology, between our "representations" (*Vorstellungen*). Kant argued that if we want to be justified in making judgments beyond our actual human experience—if we want to be justified in enunciating natural laws à la Isaac Newton—then these relations must transcend experience, not derive from it. In the analytical part of his *Critique of Pure Reason*, he mobilized an intricate sequence of arguments to show that the relations stated in natural laws are in fact relations that hold between the concepts of our understanding and the manifold that is given to us in time and space. They are not acquired from experience because their generality and necessity can, by definition, not be experienced; instead, self-generated concepts—the categories of the understanding—shape the manifold and thus make experience possible in the first place.

James does not dispute that concepts articulate our experience, but that the work of relation they perform is purely logical, transcendental, prior to experience. On the contrary, he argues, these relations can be felt: "*So surely as relations between objects exist* in rerum natura, *so surely, and more surely, do feelings exist to which these relations are known* . . . We ought to say a feeling of *and*, a feeling of *if*, a feeling of *but*, and a feeling of *by*, quite as readily as we say a feeling of blue or a feeling of cold" (*Briefer Course*, 161–162, italics in the original).

Kantians would be—and were—horrified by the idea that one could "feel" the categorical relations between our ideas. And yet, after he had generalized "feeling" into "experiencing" in his later texts, this is what makes James's empiricism radical in the *mūla* (root) sense of Nāgārjuna: he does not, like empiricists before and after him, throw up his hands when asked to explain the continuity of our experience but expands the field of experience to include relations. Experience to him is no longer a subordinate layer of cognition, awaiting articulation by concepts; instead, it extends to the categories, to the self, to all aspects of human life—it is all there is.

Drawing on his psychological research as well as on his investigation of religious experiences and his reading of French philosophy (culminating in his friendship with Henri Bergson), in his late *Essays* James draws the bewildering outlines of "A World of Pure Experience." In this world, knowing—the relation that has shaped and threatened the status of experience in so many ways—turns out to be only a specific, refined experience in which one part of an experience, the subjective side, relates to, and thus codepends on, another part of an experience as its object of knowing: "My thesis is that if we start with the supposition that there is only one primal stuff or material in the world, a stuff of which everything is composed, and if we call that stuff 'pure experience,' then knowing can easily be explained as a particular sort of relation towards one another into which portions of pure experience may enter" ("A World of Pure Experience," 1142).

There is no need to install a permanent entity like "consciousness" that initiates, controls, and reflects on the processes of knowing, except for ease of address in institutional and social settings that require it; James's arguments here sound more Buddhistic even than those of Nāgārjuna and Nietzsche. "Below" knowing is an infinitely graduated field of experiences—doubting, guessing, reading, playing—that can be articulated by conjunctive and disjunctive relations of more or less "intimacy" with the bodily core of experience. All are real experiences in the sense that they have conditioning power in the real world. The elimination of gaps between experiences, the fringing and bleeding of experiences into one another, the vision of an infinite ocean of experience from which repeated experiences emerge like temporary islands—these make up James's version of Nāgārjuna's axiom of dependent origination.

In its fully realized "radical" state, James's empiricism dissolves all that is solid into the flux of experience. The room he sits in is the experience the house made through its design and furnishing; the experience of the paper he is writing on reaches back millions of years to the earth's fauna and later to the invention of paper machines (and their engineers and workers). The book he is reading is composed of the paper and its experience, of the experience of the author, of the experience of the bookseller, and so forth. There are no discrete objects and subjects, only experiences in a specific state of reification. What looks to us like a stone is just a very slow-moving experience of the earth. This dissolving gaze will allow us to understand reading as the intersection of two singular experiences, that of the reader and that of the book. It justifies the nonmetaphorical proposition that the book has agency.

With his claim that "relations that connect experiences must themselves be experienced relations" ("A World of Pure Experience," 1160), James vaulted over the difficulties that had stumped traditional empiricists and pushed Kant and his followers into their idealist stance. Already the *Briefer Course* had given examples for the experience of cognitive halos that surround such sensations as trying to remember a name: "The rhythm of a lost word may be there without a sound to clothe it; or the evanescent sense of something which is the initial vowel or consonant may mock us fitfully, without growing more distinct" (163). In the late essays, James more boldly invokes the experiences of "with, near, next, like, from, towards, against, because, through,

for, my" ("A World of Pure Experience," 1161) that help us connect our own experiences.

Such knowing, it is true, can never aspire to the a priori certainty Newton's science had required, and Kant believed he had
furnished: "It is, the reader will see, the reinstatement of the
vague and inarticulate to its proper place in our mental life which
I am anxious to press on the attention" (*Briefer Course*, 164).
However, despite its emphasis on feeling and experience, radical
empiricism is rigorously experimental and scientific. James could
combine striving for exactitude with acknowledging vagueness
because like Nietzsche he had access to a resource unknown to
Kant and Hegel: evolutionary time. The discoveries of Charles
Lyell and Charles Darwin had opened a narrow window of time
(the Comte de Buffon in 1780 was sharply criticized for extend-
ing the age of the earth to 75,000 years) onto a vast temporal
expanse in which regularities once deemed explicable only by
assuming divine laws—such as the fixity of species—now have
the time to evolve and self-select over eons. The vague is not the
antithesis but the precursor of the exact. Western philosophy's
imperative to "save the phenomena," it turns out, had been forced
upon us by the tight time frame into which the dogma of creation had squeezed the world. Once these spatial and temporal
limitations were lifted, it became conceivable not only that species, that the solar system, that the universe had evolved, but
also that human habits, ways of sensing and perceiving, and ultimately the concepts of knowledge and truth themselves have
emerged over time. "Knowledge thus lives inside the tissue of
experience. It is *made*, and made by relations that unroll themselves in time" ("A World of Pure Experience," 1167).

Rather than looking backward to secure truth by re-cognition,
for James truth is always in the future. In an image marvelously
anticipating the culture of surfing he writes: "We live, as it were,
upon the front edge of an advancing wave-crest, and our sense
of a determinate direction in falling forward is all we cover of
the future of our path" ("A World of Pure Experience," 1172).

This—the futurity of truth—is the essence of what James and others call pragmatism. His sometime collaborator Charles Sanders Peirce went so far as to argue that the universe itself makes open-ended experiences, that its present state—for example our solar system, the number of planets and the planes of their orbits—is simply its current experience; the idea of immutable "laws" governing it results from us mistaking a brief-aperture snapshot of a constantly evolving system for its essence.

If conjunctions and disjunction, if relations can be felt, the danger arises that philosophy and psychology drown in emotions. Feelings, however, are not emotions. In the *Briefer Course* and in an important separate essay, James proposed a strikingly original view of emotions. Feelings—for example the feeling of "with-ness" or "and-ness" or "because"—are authentic, if preconceptual, modes of experience that reach for, but often fail to achieve, expression. Emotions, by contrast, are snap judgments masquerading as experiences; they presuppose a subject that sorts through experiences and pairs them with previously established templates. The traditional view that takes emotions for primary psychic events rather than for post hoc judgments aligns with the stance of re-cognizing sameness in phenomena—recognizing the planet in the moving blob—that we have identified as elemental to Western metaphysics; here, it imposes recognitive sameness on the undetermined and always novel flux of experiences. Because we do not want to make each experience anew—or because we fear that we lack the time—we reach for prior judgments and declare them immediate reactions.

James realized that radical empiricism was vulnerable to the proliferation of emotional judgments. The James-Lange theory of emotions, therefore, reverses the commonly accepted sequence in which emotions are the direct response to an external stimulus. For instance, it is not the case that we see a bear, become afraid, and then tremble, or that we lose all our money, feel sorrow, and then cry. Rather, we see the bear, our heart races, and we interpret that as fear; or we lose all our money, go into shock and cry, and then feel sorrow. Even more poignantly, we are afraid *because* we tremble, we grieve *because* we cry—emotions are interpretations of bodily events, the "mental" side of perceptions in strong experiences. James's central argument for his hypothesis was the observation that if we were to abstract them from their bodily manifestations—from the trembling and the crying—nothing of the associated emotions would remain. Fear is not fear if our heart rate stays the same.

Though James formulated this theory well before he announced his turn to radical empiricism, and although it focuses primarily on intense perceptions resulting in noticeable bodily manifestations, we can see how it advances his broader project of depersonalizing experiences and the habits and reactions we form around them. Inserting the physiological reaction between the event and the emotional response deprives the latter of its naturalness, its inevitability. Though in the majority of cases we will experience fear at the sight of a bear, it is not inconceivable that we may be simply surprised, or excited (if we are hunters), or relieved (if we are researchers). This variability increases if the event is less drastic—without being shocked, we have more space and time to reflect on the appropriateness of our emotional response.

In James's view, then, it is entirely meaningful to say, "I don't know how I feel about this book," because the task of a feeling's articulation lies yet ahead. Emotions, on the other hand, are judgments based on past judged experiences—"I love spy novels (because I read them before and enjoyed them)"; they thrive on identification. Feelings embody openness and singularity whereas emotions presuppose identity and selfhood. James's rejection of the traditional supremacy of emotions as authentic expressions of inner experiences stems from his conviction—expressed throughout the *Psychology* and implicit in the later *Essays*—that the human body is in a continuous sentient relation to its surroundings even when these relations remain below the threshold of language. This is not unlike Sigmund Freud's contemporaneous argument that conscious decisions are driven by unconscious bodily processes—though James rejects the genital focus: religious life, for example, "depends just as much upon the spleen, the pancreas, and the kidneys as on the sexual apparatus."

The thesis that relations between experiences can themselves be experienced is crucial for James's claim about the absoluteness of experience. It is a difficult thesis to prove, especially if corroboration cannot primarily come—as would be the practice of later radical empiricists such as Bataille and Deleuze—from paranormal or pathological sources. How can one show that between two states there are always intervening phases, that no experience is irreducible, solid, impenetrable? How can one articulate the experience of "with, near, next, like, from, towards, against, because, through, for, my"?

Beginning in April 1867, James spent a transformative year and a half in Germany. Originally intended as a study trip to meet post-Kantian psychologists in Berlin and Heidelberg, like so many study trips it was derailed and turned into a year of encounters and deep reading in German science and literature. The author to whom he returned again and again was Johann Wolfgang von Goethe. He knew of him, of course, from Emerson's Goethe essay in the collection *Representative Men*, and from the transcendentalists' fascination with Goethe, for which Emerson, again, was a central figure. Importantly, the transcendentalists appreciated Goethe both as a poet and as a scientist, whereas in Germany's post-Kantian universities his scientific writings were belittled or simply not read.

Goethe considered his most important contribution to the natural sciences to be the concept of metamorphosis. It sought to capture the transitional stages of change in a plant or an animal while holding on to the notions of identity in change, and to an ideal form toward which all changes tended. Metamorphosis "saved" the phenomena of change while preventing the natural world from drifting apart into formless contingency. If only we develop a poetic mindset that extends our attention span, Goethe argued in treatises, poems, notebooks, and conversations, we can account for all the apparent gaps between forms, and we can discern that their change follows rules and tends toward an ideal order. Proper attention and imaginative experimentation will show the relations between seemingly distinct phases and states in a changing phenomenon, between leaf and bud in a plant, for example, or between seemingly separate natural realms, for example between stones, stalks, and bones.

Even during his lifetime Goethe lamented that his theories were misunderstood and disrespected by the scientific establishment. What the professors lacked, he contended, was the poetic sensibility required to see the intervening stages that emerged in the cracks between their coarse concepts. In Goethe's polemics there is a subtle play with the German word for poet, *Dichter*. While commonly derived from the Latin word for "to dictate" (*dictare*), in German it resonates with the adjective *dicht* (tight, dense, compact) that can also function as a preposition: "close by, near." A *Dichter* by this etymology is someone who brings things closer (*dichter*) together, who discerns their closeness and finds words for their relation.

Goethe's oeuvre pulses with poetic expressions of relations. His poems derive their force—aside from technical mastery—from his uncanny ability to articulate the experience of relations: distance, closeness, togetherness, nearness, absence, or presence, but also the relations of attending, of parting, of expecting, of fearing, of gazing, of beholding.

However, the relation that most captivated Goethe and that he attempted to express in poetry, drama, and prose is the one Kant deemed so abstract that it could only be understood on a logical, transcendental level: "because." The German equivalent *weil* has a verbal form, *weilen*, that conveys being present, tarrying, lingering, or, indeed, whiling. Its nominal form, *die Weile*, denotes the time that passes between, separates, and at the same time connects events. When combined with the infamous prefix *ver-*, *verweilen* is used to indicate the lingering in time, at a place, or on a topic in conversation. As its antonym, rhyming poets often use *eilen* (hurrying); "haste makes waste" in German turns into "Eile mit Weile." The affect melancholia becomes, in the nineteenth century, "long whiling," *Langeweile*, ennui, boredom.

Goethe's fascination with the relational qualities of *weil* lasted throughout his life. It is legible, for example, in the fifteenth of his Roman Elegies, in which he adds to the well-known palindrome of *roma-amor* the anagram *mora*, delay or deferment (as in moratorium), the Latin word for *Weile*. The lovers in the poem experience all the joys and all the agonies encapsulated in the *weil*, showing the depth and intensity with which conjunctive and disjunctive relations can be experienced. Goethe goes so far as to suggest that it is the moratorium, the act of lingering and deferring, that causes love to grow rather than be thwarted. To deny the experience of this causing, for Goethe and for James, amounts to denying the complexity of the experience "love."

This fascination with the relation *weil*, in which time and causation are not yet differentiated, became the driving force of Goethe's lifelong project, the drama of Faust. As a good Kantian, Faust wagers with the devil that he would never desire to linger in the in-between moments of chasing his desires. "If I ever say to a moment in time ["Augenblick"] / 'stay a while ["verweile"], you are so beautiful' / then you may put me into chains / then I am ready to perish." *Faust* unfolds over thousands of verses as a search for the elusive experience of this time-before-causation. Whether Goethe's proposed solution—finding the ultimate cause in the "eternal feminine"—is a satisfying conclusion remains a subject of debate.

Goethe did not rely solely on the poetic resonance of the single word *weil* to capture the experience of relation; he also explored it in narrative prose. The concept of *Bildung*—the idea of education or formation, which propels his second novel, *Wilhelm Meister's Apprenticeship* (1795–1796)—is, like metamorphosis, an attempt to join change and identity, to make the stages of a character's development readable against a background of change. *Bildung* stands for the continuity of purpose and individual maturation of a character and encompasses both psychological growth and aesthetic harmony. Although it remains questionable whether Goethe succeeded with his program—the novel ends abruptly with a deus ex machina contraption—the concept proved so powerful as a descriptor of narrative development that it is hard to find a novel of the nineteenth century to which the designation bildungsroman has not been affixed.

Of course, had James really wanted to bolster his claim that all relations can be experienced with examples from literature, he might have looked to his brother's work. Henry James's writing is (in)famously preoccupied with such states of mind as expectation, suspicion, premonition, jealousy, and disappointment (or, inversely, naivete, trust, innocence, and kindness) that lead characters to endlessly puzzle about the relation between events, between people, between objects. If ever there was a *Dichter* in the sense discussed—an expert in drawing things closer and to articulate the relation between them—it was Henry James. Much to the chagrin of his brother's sturdier literary tastes, Henry James seemed to understand that if one just looks closely enough, one could see that a character's experiences co-originate in the intersection of myriad conditions, and that the *Dichter*'s task is to bring as many of them to language as possible.

The oft-repeated complaints about Henry James's fastidious late style react to the temporary loss of narrative ground, to the disorientation that befalls the reader who struggles to distinguish reflection from locution, imagination from representation, narrated from narrative space, to say nothing of the meandering syntax that warps sentences in the same way as the plot warps the story. Yet while it is disorienting, it is also liberating to read Henry James's late work. He may well be the first novelist to make the reading of experiences coincide with the experience of reading. Both are slow processes that take time and attention and balance, just like surfing in the metaphor William deployed so poignantly.

Since the end of the nineteenth century—since the end of the period known as literary realism when other media of representation had encroached (photography) or were beginning to encroach (film) on its monopoly of representing experience—

reading novels no longer merely acquaints the reader with experiences but becomes itself an experience, perhaps the experience of experiences par excellence.

WHAT HAVE WE LEARNED from these three apostles of experience? Nāgārjuna, Nietzsche, and William James—each in their own way but overlapping to a surprising and mutually illuminating degree—analyze, expand, and show ways to overcome our subject-centered, dualistic understanding of experience.

Nāgārjuna delimits the field of experience in the most radical way possible: by simply not heeding the Western (and Brahmin) imperative to impose meaning on the world. Instead, he takes embodied human experience as the sole framework for evaluating knowledge and truth, focusing intently on the intricacies and conceptual fallacies into which unguarded experience leads. With no firm ground to stand on, Nāgārjuna argues that the mind, individually and collectively, generates fictions and conventions that it then forgets having generated. The *MMK* run through a catalogue of such fictions, taking their intention seriously but showing that they all are logically and intrinsically flawed or, to use the Mahāyāna term, that they are empty. Importantly, the path out of this web of fictions and reified beliefs is through logic and analysis, not faith or conversion. Unlike for modern critics of reification and ideology, however, Nāgārjuna offers no stable parameter—conceptual or economic reality, for example, or human nature—against which to measure the truth of these fictions and conventions. Instead, the goal of enlightened experiences is to recognize their emptiness and to engage with them honestly and compassionately.

Nietzsche arrives at the same position, but from within the Western logic of cosmodicy and theodicy. He charts historical trajectories, names the cast of characters, and assails the logic of fictions the West believes as foundational truths. His focus is on the fusion between Christianity and social control (and not, importantly, on the message of Jesus), and on the lasting harm these fictions have inflicted on our capacity for genuine experience. Like the Buddha, Nietzsche awakens to the truth of a world without entrenched views and the adjustments it requires from us; like the Buddha he realizes that escape from the strictures of justification is possible only into an infinitely—eternally—conditioned world; like the Buddha, he—in the figure of Zarathustra—struggles in the drama of communicating a radically experiential insight.

William James, in turn, synthesizes Nāgārjuna's panfictionalism and Nietzsche's diagnosis of modernity and tests them in empirical research and in his explorations of extreme forms of experience. Under the microscope of his analyses, raw, "pure" states of experience become visible—states in which the fictions of subject and object, sensations and concept, other and self are, at best, embryonic. His exposure to modern forms of fiction—to the novel in particular—allows him to see what Nāgārjuna could not: a way to experience the experience of others through reading, and thus to dispel the aura of solitude that hovers both over the Buddhistic meditator and the "solitary Wanderer" 6,000 feet above sea level.

It is to the reading of experience, to the experience of the novel that we now turn. My argument will be that the modern novel, for generic and historical reasons, meets the requirements of genuine experience to which our three witnesses have testified: that it be unbounded by ontological and epistemological limitations, that it recognize yet take seriously the fictitious nature of conventions (including the conventions of narrative), that it be open to the radical novelty of its explorations, and that the field of experience must be extended to nonhuman experiencers. With Nāgārjuna in mind, I want to investigate how the modern novel acquaints its readers with the facility for handling the conventional truth-fiction divide; with Nietzsche, I want to show how the modern novel became an instrument of conformist education; and with William James I want to explore how the experience of reading becomes the experience that we can, despite all obstacles, share in common.

Bibliographical Essay

The literature on James is, deservedly, near-infinite. Coming to James from the "outside" (from idealist and deconstructive philosophies, from a European context, from a primary interest in literature) I found the following sources extremely helpful: Louis Menand, *The Metaphysical Club: A Story of Ideas in America* (New York: Farrar, Straus and Giroux, 73–148); David Lapoujade, *William James: Empiricism and Pragmatism* (Durham, NC: Duke University Press, 2019); Felicitas Krämer, *Erfahrungsvielfalt und Wirklichkeit: Zu William James' Realitätsverständnis* (Göttingen: Vandenhoeck & Ruprecht 2006); the essays in Sarin Marchetti, ed., *The Jamesian Mind* (London: Routledge, 2022), especially David Scott, "James and the 'East': Buddhism and Japan" (333–343) and Rachel Christy, "'The Moral Earth, Too, Is Round': James and Nietzsche on the Aim of Philosophy" (385–397); and Calvin O. Schrag, "Struktur der Erfahrung in der Philosophie von James und Whitehead," *Zeitschrift für philosophische Forschung* 23, no. 4 (1969): 479–494, especially 481–484.

A very circumspect assessment of James's role in American philosophy of the nineteenth century is by Cornel West, *The American Evasion of Philosophy* (Madison: University of Wisconsin Press, 1989), 54–68. James's reflections on the potential and dangers of introspection are articulated in "On Some Omissions of Introspective Psychology," in William James, *Writings, 1878–1899* (New York: Library of America, 1992), 986–1013. The reflections on "The Stream of Consciousness" are in William James, *Psychology: Briefer Course*, in *Writings, 1878–1899*, 152–173. He speaks about fringing on pages 162–166. *"A permanently existing 'idea' which makes its appearance before the footlights of consciousness at periodical intervals is as mythological an entity as the Jack of Spades,"* in James, *Psychology*, 157 (italics in the original).

I have embedded Kant's argument for the "epigenetic" origins of our categories in contemporary debates about biological reproduction in my *Self-Generation: Biology, Philosophy, and Literature around 1800* (Stanford, CA: Stanford University Press, 1997), 48–64. The essay "A World of Pure Experience" is in William James, *Writings, 1902–1910* (New York: Library of America, 1987), 1159–1182. It forms, together with "Does 'Consciousness' Exist?" (1141–1158) and "The Experience of Activity" (an appendix to his lecture series "A Pluralistic Universe" [797–812]), the clearest statement of the stakes of radical empiricism. James defines "pure experience" as the "instant field of the present" ("Does 'Consciousness' Exist?," 1151), i.e., experience before it is sorted and shaped by concepts, norms, or habits—pure potentiality. "Does 'Consciousness' Exist?" (1145–1147) also contains the clearest statement that everything (room, book, man) is an experience. At the end of "Does 'Consciousness' Exist?" (1157) James comes, unknowingly, around to an authentic Buddhist insight: "Breath, which was ever the original 'spirit,' breath moving outwards, between the glottis and the nostrils, is, I am persuaded, the essence out of which philosophers have constructed the entity known to them as consciousness."

For the interesting debate around Buffon and the age of the earth, see Noah Heringman, *Deep Time: A Literary History* (Princeton, NJ: Princeton University Press, 2023), 75–119. Charles Sanders Peirce's view of the current state of the solar system as its current experience is in "Design and Chance," in *Writings of Charles S. Peirce: A Chronological Edition*, ed. Christian J. W. Kloesel, vol. 4, *1879–1884* (Bloomington: Indiana University Press, 1989), 544–554. For James's theory of emotions, see his *Briefer Course*, 350–365, and "What Is an Emotion?" in *Mind* (April 1884): 188–205. For a recent interpretation of this approach, see Shannon Sullivan, "William James on Emotion: Physiology and/as Spirituality," in Marchetti, *The Jamesian Mind*, 61–69. This is also, broadly speaking, the Buddhist view of emotions. Whereas Christian ethics acknowledges the primacy of emotions but sorts them as either noxious or propitious for salvation (e.g., envy vs. compassion), Buddhist treatises, like James's, understand emotions as (mis)interpretations of occurrences (frustration over their impermanence). Very different ethics result from these different approaches. See, for example, Shantideva, *The Way of the Bodhisattva* (Boston: Shambala Publications, 2011), chapter 6, "Patience." James confesses his ignorance of, and sympathy for, Buddhism in the postscript of "The Varieties of Religious Experience," in *Writings, 1902–1910*, 466.

For a systematic account of the similarity between Nāgārjuna's and James's thought, see David Kalupahana, "The Epistemology of William James and Early Buddhism," in *Religious Experience, Religious Belief*, ed. John Runzo and Craig Ihara (Lanham, MD: University Press of America, 1986), 53–73.

James's quip about Freudian theories of sexuality is in "The Varieties of Religious Experience," 1911. James would meet Freud and Carl Jung at Clark University in 1909. One of the purposes of James's early visit to

Germany in 1868 was to get a closer look at the theory and practice of German experimental psychology; much of his later work is, often explicitly, directed against its binarisms and data fetishism. For the emergence and importance of the graphical method in German science, see Cornelius Borck, *Brainwaves: A Cultural History of Electroencephalography* (London: Routledge, 2018), and Cornelius Borck, "The 'German Question' in the History of Science and the 'Science Question' in German History," *German History* 29, no. 4 (2011): 628–639. The intermediary figure between James and the German physical psychologists is Hugo Münsterberg, a student of Wilhelm Wundt's who ended up directing the psychology lab at Harvard; see Henning Schmidgen, "Münsterberg's Photoplays: Instruments and Models in His Laboratories at Freiburg and Harvard (1891–1893)," *The Virtual Laboratory*, 2008, https://vlp.mpiwg-berlin.mpg.de/essays/data/art71; and R. M. Brain, "Self-Projection: Hugo Münsterberg on Empathy and Oscillation in Cinema Spectatorship," *Science in Context* 25, no. 3 (2012): 329–353.

The importance of Goethe for the transcendentalists, and for Emerson, is hard to overstate; for a recent analysis, see Kai Sina, "Goethe," in *Kollektivpoetik: Zu einer Literatur der offenen Gesellschaft in der Moderne mit Studien zu Goethe, Emerson, Whitman und Thomas Mann* (Berlin: De Gruyter, 2020), 109–144. For the concept of metamorphosis, see Eva Geulen, *Aus dem Leben der Form: Goethes Morphologie und die Nager* (Berlin: August Verlag, 2016). See also Goethe's didactic poem "Die Metamorphose der Pflanzen," in Johann Wolfgang Goethe, *Gedichte, 1756–1799* (Frankfurt: Deutscher Klassiker Verlag, 1998), 639–641. For the rejection of Goethean science by the German academic establishment, see Eva Axer, Eva Geulen, and Alexandra Heimes, *Aus dem Leben der Form: Studien zum Nachleben von Goethes Morphologie in der Theoriebildung des 20. Jahrhunderts* (Göttingen: Wallstein, 2021), 32–34. James met with the two scientists most responsible for this rejection, Hermann von Helmholtz and Emil Du Bois-Reymond, in Berlin.

For a detailed list of James's repeated reading and studying of Goethe, see Alexandra Strohmaier, *Poetischer Pragmatismus: Goethe und William James* (Berlin: de Gruyter, 2019), 74–79; for the similarity of James's and Goethe's understanding of external relations, see 182–185. Goethe's "Wirkung in die Ferne" or "Nähe des Geliebten" are among the innumerable poems that speak of the interstices of experience; the sense that Goethe invokes to capture these transitions is *ahnen* (guessing, suspecting, sensing). (The poems are in, respectively, *Gedichte 1800–1832* [132] and *Gedichte, 1756–1799* [647]; both Frankfurt: Deutscher Klassiker Verlag, 1998.) The famous scene in which Faust wagers his soul is in Goethe's *Faust* (Frankfurt: Deutscher Klassiker Verlag, 1999), verse 1700, 76. For the temporality of whiling, see Joseph Vogl, *On Tarrying* (Chicago: University of Chicago Press, 2019). The French *causer* means both causing and idly chatting. Goethe's *Wilhelm Meister's Apprenticeship* in Thomas Carlyle's translation was of signal importance for the transcendentalists and the generation following. David Lapoujade, *Fictions du Pragmatisme* (Paris: Minuit, 2008) reads Henry James's entire oeuvre as a demonstration of radical empiricism. Broader in its scope but equally incisive is Paul Grimstadt, *Experience and Experimental Writing: Literary Pragmatism from Emerson to the Jameses* (Oxford: Oxford University Press, 2013), 90–119. Here is a snippet of a conversation from one of Henry James's stories: "'What great fact?' 'The fact of a relation. The adventure's the relation; the relation's an adventure. The romance, the novel, the drama are the picture of one.'" Henry James, "The Story in It," in *Complete Stories, 1898–1910* (New York: The Library of America, 1996), 41.

For the relation of James' Radical Empiricism to both Buddhism and to C. S. Pierce, see Dan Arnold, "Pragmatism as Transcendental Philosophy, Part 1: Pierce in Light of James's Radical Empiricism," *American Journal of Theology & Philosophy* 42 no. 1 (2021): 50–103.

Chapter 5 | **The Reading of Experience**

Horace, the popularizer of Aristotle and the author of the most influential treatise on poetics in the West, proclaimed that poets, like orators, should seek not only to instruct and be useful but also delight. Setting standards that would endure for centuries, he stipulated that such delight and entertainment could only come from epic, dramatic, and lyric poetry. Though the Greeks had produced fantastical adventure novels and the Romans would imitate them in this area as well, Horatian poetics could not—and would not for centuries—accommodate the shapeless prose of the novel, to say nothing of the ancient novel's erratic plot development and its often undistinguished characters. Emerging from a convergence of myth, oratory, elegy, and comedy, the ancient novel literalized the notion of ex-perience: heroes and heroines who incessantly travel, flee, err, are kidnapped, are rescued—who move through space and cross boundaries.

Delight and entertainment through reading were problematic features still in the seventeenth and eighteenth centuries. On one hand, they polluted the air of sophistication that an increasingly secular culture valued as signs of intellectual and social distinction. On the other, nonprofessional reading remained largely confined to the Bible, which, the Song of Songs notwithstanding, has very little to offer in terms of delight and sheer entertainment. Early attempts to portray Jesus as a conquering hero in the mold of Jason or Hercules were quickly quashed by the church fathers who drew a strict line between edification and entertainment. The conversion stories that punctuate Christian apologetics—Augustine picking up the letters of Saint Paul, Petrarch opening *The Confessions* atop Mont Ventoux, each chancing on a passage that seems to speak directly to their circumstances—emphasize that the narrative place of a biblical episode is secondary to its moral significance.

From a narratological point of view, the Bible is the ultimate realist narrative: its beginning and its end align with the beginning and end of its subject matter—the created world. The fact that both the genesis and the apocalypse of the world could be narrated prepared readers to accept both the utter unreality of an omniscient narrator and the realism of what was being narrated. Combined with the expectation that every word and every pericope referred to something that had not simply factual but paradigmatic relevance, Bible reading in many ways conditioned lay readers for the experience of the novel.

The divinity and paradigmatic depth of the Bible required specific modes of reading to uncover its layers of meaning. Manuals of Christian interpretation stipulated that since the richness of the divine word could be captured only imperfectly in the vessels of human language, a quadrangle of "senses" would be needed to define the area of its interpretation. One side was the materiality of language and the sequence of events—the *sensus literalis* or *historicus* that would later spawn the disciplines of philology and history. In the Bible, furthermore, events relate to one another, often across long intervals, as foreshadowing and fulfillment; the simple forward direction of the story is countered by the *sensus allegoricus* that imbues every passage with additional meaning and turns, importantly for Christian apologetics, the Hebrew Bible into the Old Testament. Drawing this second side of the quadrangle requires a different skill set but has the element of learning in common with the first. The third side, the *sensus tropologicus* or *moralis*, appeals to the individual reader who must learn to align their life experiences with the experiences depicted, transforming textual meaning into personal guidance. Note that in this relation, the reader's experience is supposed to be molded *after* the experience described and is thus confined to the area enclosed by the quadruple sense. Closing the square, the *sensus anagogicus* allows sufficiently inspired and learned theologians to speculate what a specific passage might tell us about the history of salvation and where in its unfolding we may find ourselves.

However secular we claim to be, it is not difficult to recognize the persistence of these senses in contemporary literary studies, both academic and extra-academic. The 1970s and 1980s, for example, saw a return to the first two senses, in an effort to scrub from the teaching of literature its moralistic and empathetic focus. At the same time, the anagogical sense—the philosophical study of the history of literature à la György Lukács and Fredric Jameson—has continued to provide a salvific, if secular, frame for these close readings.

Excluded from the canon of respectable genres and overshadowed by the normativity of religious experience and its codification in morality tales, the novel as a medium of secular experience began to thrive in the seventeenth century. Experience, we have seen, had been discounted both by religious orthodoxy that had always been uneasy with claims of mystical experience and by a rational philosophy that wanted to secure the foundations of human knowledge against the encroachment of theology. Attempts from René Descartes to Immanuel Kant to find a secure foothold for human knowledge, atheistic as they pretended to be, still agreed with religious orthodoxy that experience—often equated with the sensory perceptions of the body—was an unreliable guide to understanding the divinity of God as well as nature and its laws. In the absence of divine guarantees for knowledge, only the self-certainty of the knowing mind and its cognitive rules—Kant's "I think"—could provide the unshakable foundation modern science needed.

The novel, however, turned its banishment from religious edification, cognitive respectability, and canonic beauty into an advantage. Its formlessness became its capaciousness: it could include—and in the Romantic era regularly did include—poems and poetic situations, while from drama it absorbed the practice of uncommented dialogue. It provoked the readers' trained moral sense by showing its protagonists do the wrong thing again and again, with often only a perfunctory deathbed conversion toward standard virtue. And it unsettled the theological and philosophical notion of creation and authorship by playing with a particular framing device: the pretense that the narrative, as a manuscript, a cache of letters, or a diary had fallen into the hands of the author-editor who simply edited, and at most commented on, the narrative. This framing device, seemingly accidental and peripheral, cannot be overestimated in its importance for the experience of the novel. After the tone-setting example of Miguel de Cervantes's *Don Quixote* (1605 and 1615), all of these novels used the same device: Daniel Defoe's *Robinson Crusoe* (1719), Jonathan Swift's *Gulliver's Travels* (1726), Voltaire's *Candide* (1759), and the deluge of epistolary novels by Samuel Richardson (*Pamela*, 1740), Jean-Jacques Rousseau (*Julie*, 1761), Pierre Choderlos de Laclos (*Les liaisons dangereuses*, 1782), and Johann Wolfgang von Goethe (*The Sufferings of Young Werther*, 1774).

The proximate, real-world function of the fictitious editor was to evade censorship and personal accountability, regardless of whether such self-distancing would hold up in the judicial reality of the seventeenth and eighteenth centuries. In this respect, the device mirrors the Enlightenment practice of printing risqué and seditious books abroad and then reimporting them with impunity into their country of origin. At the same time, however, there were distinct formal advantages to this encapsulation: claiming to have ventured upon the narrative as an object in time and space conferred a specific kind of realism on the novel—a realism not of the story told but of its having been told. This move deflected attention from recognizing signs of authorial craft—the introduction and characterization of protagonists, the scope and depth of descriptions, the disposition of dialogues, the division into chapters and books, and so forth—at a time when the novel had not yet owned up to "the art of fiction." For readers until the end of the eighteenth century, today's primary question of realism—could this story really have happened?—was muffled by the secondary realism of the found-manuscript device: yes, this manuscript could really have been found.

This deflection of authorship is a pivotal moment in the rise of the novel as the premier medium of experience. It accords experience to the book itself, be it a found manuscript or a cache of letters; it situates the book as a fragment of experience in the same world as the readers', it removes the author as an intermediary and thus confronts readers—trained in their Bible study to identify with the hero or the heroine—with the passionate and tragic vicissitudes of figures in their own space of experience, however distant it may be. To be sure, this was a gradual process with many different components—gender being one of them—but the reports about the staggering impact the epistolary novels of Richardson, of Rousseau, and a little later, of Goethe had on unsuspecting male and female readers show that this new reading of experience was both overwhelming and utterly addictive. It is this realism of the reading experience that carries the novel's success, not the degree of verisimilitude or the self-ennobling statements authors made to find acceptance among the critics.

The irony often associated with the modern novel has its discursive roots in this self-distancing of authors from their work. In the first half of the nineteenth century, when the fictional editor morphed into the omniscient narrator, readers were still regularly addressed with stage directions to help the narrative along: "we now leave our young protagonist and turn to . . ." Preserved in this gesture is the fiction that there *is* something to turn away from—but now it is not the (fictional) materiality of the found manuscript but a reality of events that the novel claims to convey and that the author arranges for our view.

This sense of realism is not the only consequence of the fictional editor device. When Cervantes, at the end of the first book of *Don Quixote*, interrupted the description of a sword fight because the manuscript he purported to be editing had run out and he needed to scour the bazaars for its sequel, he activated two interrelated features that shaped the novel for centuries.

The first is the manufacture of suspense. Unlike the Bible or other Christian narratives, which lack suspense because their end—temporal and moral—is preordained, the novel thrives on uncertainty. Suspense is entirely human; it is a feature of the openness and unpredictability of human experience that must be unknown to God's omniscient perspective. Like every novelist after him, Cervantes knew that suspense is born of interruption, and that the best way to create such interruptions is to make use of the segmentations inherent in the medium of the printed book. The divisions between chapters, between books, or between volumes introduce "real" interruptions that manifest in readers' lives. The eager anticipation for the next installment or volume is another instance where the "reality effect" of the novel is not constricted to practices of representation but reaches into the affective and daily life of its readers.

The manufacture of suspense through editorial interruptions reveals a second important feature of the modern novel: its seriability. Fictional editors with their backstories make serial publication narratively plausible, regardless of whether a novel is actually published in installments or not. In the interruption they create the very continuity that is being interrupted and serialized. Changing the setting in a new chapter, jumping across the timeline, introducing new characters—all the elements associated with the author's craft of plotting—are made possible by the assurance of the editor that the narrative we are reading is continuous. This fictional continuity in the narrative of the novel mirrors the experience of the readers whose lives also continue beyond the focus of their immediate attention. Characters in a novel are "real" not simply because of the author's art of characterization but because readers suppose they get on with their lives—or die, as was the case with Nell in Charles Dickens's *The Old Curiosity Shop*—in the time between segments.

When in the 1830s this potential for serialization was actualized, the lives of the novel and the lives of the readers intersected in ever more vivid ways. The novel makes singular experiences during its publication in response to its reception, just as the reader changes in the absorption and rumination over the narrative they are reading. The novel's representation of experience—of a protagonist's drawn-out adventures in time and space—is met in the experience of representation, of drawn-out publication schedules, and in the drawn-out experience of reading.

These features of the novel, present from its inception, developed their full potential because the corresponding web of industrial, cultural, and social conditions came into place—increased literacy, shorter workdays, artificial lighting, endless paper, rotary printing, laxer censorship, to name the most important. Because this web became so strong, the fictitious editor was no longer needed and replaced by a new, equally fictitious, equally improbable figure, the omniscient narrator. The omniscient voice is as "unrealistic" as the fictitious editor—who is this person that knows the story from so many different angles, and from inside of so many minds?—but its interventions become less drastic, at times detectable only in a spurious "we" or in acts of recall the diegesis itself does not yield. The progressive disembodiment and ultimate disappearance of the narrating voice is not possible without the novel's industrial conditions of production and distribution—the network of authors, publishers, printers, reviewers, reading clubs, lending libraries, public readings, and so on into which the reader is inserted by the act of reading.

The genealogy of its emergence shows that the modern realist novel is a thoroughly conventional phenomenon. It is infinitely conditioned; its proximate and distant conditions can be—and have been—empirically researched and are themselves conditioned by other conditions, and so forth: in Nāgārjuna's parlance, there is no *svabhāva*, no essential cause in which the cascade of conditions terminates, however attractive it may be to assume, for example, an irrepressible need for human beings to tell and consume stories. This may or may not be so. Conditions are not producing, "causing" causes, as Nāgārjuna shows in the first chapter of *MMK*; the assumption of a first condition that causes or grounds a phenomenon leads into contradictions.

Nāgārjuna, as we have seen, decomposes the world into a network of necessary conditions while denying that there are sufficient conditions, or reasons, that, in an emphatic sense, bring about, or give ground to, phenomena. If sufficient reasons are reasons through which something comes about and necessary reasons those without which something cannot arise, then rotary printing presses, gaslights, or lending libraries make up the network of the realist novel's necessary conditions. It would be hazardous to argue that any of these conditions were sufficient for the rise of the novel, though it has been tried.

However, Western literary hermeneutics evolved, as we have seen, from its biblical predecessor, and it is because of this heritage that for the longest time the author was regarded as the sufficient reason of a novel. Considerable interpretive energies went into elucidating the relation between author and work; although this paradigm has weakened considerably, for the iconic authors of national traditions, the Goethes, Fyodor Dostoyevskys, or Marcel Prousts, it is still in full force. Even alternative approaches, such as media studies or gender studies, search for reasons that would stop conditions from proliferating. For Nāgārjuna, who never laid eyes on a novel, these are retroactive attempts to stabilize and center the groundless net of conditions; with their focus on literary authorship or other sufficient causes, interpreters inadvertently replay the metaphysical and theological drama of causation and creation as the cornerstone of a meaningful world.

More profoundly, Nāgārjuna's leveling of the barrier between truth and fiction in favor of seeing the truth of convention and the convention of truth allows for experiencing and enjoying novels unburdened by the metaphysics of representation. To pose the question whether poets lie—a dominant concern in Western aesthetics and literary theory—makes sense only under the assumption of a coherent world that predates its representation and about which lies could be told. Nāgārjuna does not deny a thought-independent reality—he is not an idealist in the mold of George Berkeley—but he denies that this reality is ordered as a world, as a cosmos, as a totality characterized by identity, repetition, and stability. For him, there is local coherence centered around lived experiences but no underlying set of relations that holds everything together.

And yet, all of Buddhism's elaborate soteriology would be for nought if this reality had no impact on human behavior and thought. The term most apt for translating this realm—ontologically empty and psychologically efficacious—into the vocabulary of the West is fiction. Only in a metaphysics with strong commitments to ontological fullness can fiction carry the aura of falsehood or secondariness. In many other views, fiction (and such avatars as Will to Power, Ideology, Language Game) is all, or most, of what there is. Fiction accentuates, in contrast to the more static "convention," the role we play in creating the world around us—our interpersonal relations, our engagement with institutions and state authority, intimacy with our body and our mortality. Only in moments of shock, of heightened awareness or intense therapy, do we see these relations as human made. Buddhist scholarship, without apparent irony, often uses the cognate Marxist term "reification" to illustrate that fiction is not the opposite of truth but the way meaning coagulates and solidifies both in individual relations (including relations to oneself) and in social contexts.

It is in our (Western) relation to narrative fictions that we accept the Buddhist codependency of truths: that the ultimate truth is that conventions are conventions, "mountains are mountains," fictions are fictions. In our reading, we accept novelistic accounts of experiences as truth while remaining aware of their thoroughly conventional nature—in fact, for the language game "novel" and "fictional narrative" to work this is exactly what we must do. There is no need, no evidence that this acceptance or suspension requires an act of the will; rather, it is the absence of any willing or any controlled epistemological labor that makes the experience of narratives so compelling.

When we read novels, we do not typically wonder whether receiving a life-altering anonymous bequest, discovering one's husband's infidelity through a crack in a bowl, waking up as a beetle or as a disembodied voice is likely or even possible—we accept, appreciate, enjoy, and puzzle over the scenarios arranged for us within the convention "novel," regardless of whether they are realistic in the stunted representational sense, or surrealist, magical, modernist, fantastical, or satirical. We read with parallax vision.

Ironically, then, it is from an Eastern tradition unaware of the conventions of the novel that we might learn to take literature seriously. The individual and social value of reading narrative fiction is not first and foremost that we acquire empathy for others and exercise the mind in the fields of the imagination; empathy, desirable though it is, identifies with another fully established subject in its struggle against the "ways of the world." The Middle Way shows that we read at a deeper level—we follow how a character emerges, changes, or perishes in the struggle to distinguish self from other, truth from convention, and relate this struggle to our own. We can make this relation because the practice of reading, as the following chapter seeks to show, is itself an experience in which the distinction of self and other is in flux.

Deep reading of secular narrative fiction latches on to a character's open-ended, failure-prone journey; often this leads into situations in which a character mistakes a convention—marriage, religious life, material success—for an essential truth that the reader recognizes as empty convention. The two sides in this experience of reading, the reader and the character, stand in a relationship similar to that between conventional and ultimate truth: while the character pursues an ultimate truth amid conventions—the truth of the self (bildungsroman) and/or the truth of the other (novels of love/adultery and ambition)—the reader can see the limitation, the emptiness of that pursuit. "Seeing," however, is not the right term, as the understanding of experience is itself an experience: the time-consuming process of reading itself.

Bibliographical Essay

For Horace and the afterlife of the *Ars Poetica*—arguably more influential than Aristotle's *Poetics*—see Leon Golden, "The Reception of Horace's *Ars Poetica*," in *A Companion to Horace*, ed. Gregson Davis (Oxford: Blackwell, 2010), 391–413. For the emergence and characteristics of the ancient novel, see Pierre Grimal, introduction to *Romans grecs et latins* (Paris: Gallimard, 1958), ix–xxvi; Niklas Holzberg, "The Genre," in *The Ancient Novel* (London: Routledge, 1994), 1–20 (with amusingly antiquated references to 1980s soap operas); Tomas Hägg, "The Ancient Greek Novel: A Single Model or a Plurality of Forms?," in *The Novel*, ed. Franco Moretti, vol. 1 (Princeton, NJ: Princeton University Press, 2006), 125–155; and Sylvie Thorel-Cailleteau, "The Poetry of Mediocrity," in *The Novel*, ed. Franco Moretti, vol. 2 (Princeton, NJ: Princeton University Press 2006), 64–94. Thomas Pavel, *La pensée du roman* (Paris: Gallimard, 2003) is very eloquent about the ancient novel and its subterranean influence.

For the formation of the New Testament in opposition to secular narratives, see Konrad Schmid and Jens Schröter, *The Making of the Bible* (Cambridge, MA: Harvard University Press, 2021), 222–279. For Jerome's and Augustine's hostility to the depiction of Jesus as an epic hero, see my "Patchwork und Poesie: Bemerkungen zum spätantiken cento," in *Denkzettel Antike: Texte zum kulturellen Vergessen*, ed. G. Treusch-Dieter (Berlin: Reimer, 1989), 229–238. For the importance of random "Bible lots" (*sortes biblicae*) as a way to individualize the universal message of the Bible, see Christopher Wild, *Descartes's Meditative Turn: Cartesian Thought as Spiritual Practice* (Stanford, CA: Stanford University Press, 2024), 56–69.

The classic (Catholic) account of scriptural exegesis is Henri de Lubac, *Medieval Exegesis: The Four Senses of Scripture* (Grand Rapids, MI: Eerdmans, 1998); see also Franklin T. Harkins, "Hugh of St. Victor: Didascalion on the Study of Reading," in *Handbuch der Bibelhermeneutiken: von Origenes bis zur Gegenwart*, ed. Oda Wischmeyer (Berlin: de Gruyter, 2016), 135–148. Fredric Jameson has actualized—with reservations, but still emphatically—the four senses for contemporary literary study in his *Allegory and Ideology* (London: Verso, 2019). For the "return to philology" and its many problems, see Merve Emre, "The Return to Philology," *PMLA* 138, no. 1 (2023): 171–177. For the emergence of philology as a self-standing discipline, see James Turner, *Philology: The Forgotten Origins of the Modern Humanities* (Princeton, NJ: Princeton University Press, 2014). For an attempt at a "deep history" of the novel, see (aside from the first volume of Moretti's *The Novel*) Steven Moore, *The Novel: An Alternative History 1600–1800* (London: Bloomsbury, 2013).

For the supreme importance of the fictional editor device, see Wolfgang Iser, *Laurence Sterne: Tristram Shandy* (Cambridge: Cambridge University Press, 1988); Uwe Wirth, *Die Geburt des Autors aus dem Geist der Herausgeberfiktion: Editoriale Rahmung im Roman um 1800: Wieland, Goethe, Brentano, Jean Paul und E.T.A. Hoffmann* (Paderborn: Brill, 2008); Derek Alsop, *Practices of Reading: Interpreting the Novel* (New York: Saint Martin's, 1999), 28–50; and especially Nicholas Paige, *Before Fiction: The Ancient Regime of the Novel* (Philadelphia: University of Pennsylvania Press, 2011).

For the philosophical and literary history of fiction, see Peter Lamarque and Stein Haugom Olsen, *Truth, Fiction, and Literature: A Philosophical Perspective* (Oxford: Clarendon, 1994); Tobias Klauk and Tilmann Köppe, eds., *Fiktionalität: Ein interdisziplinäres Handbuch* (Berlin: de Gruyter, 2014); and Johannes Franzen, Patrick Galke-Janzen, Frauke Janzen, and Marc Wurich, eds., *Geschichte der Fiktionalität: Diachrone Perspektiven auf ein kulturelles Konzept* (Baden-Baden: Nomos, 2018). The opposition between novels and science was proverbial in post-Newtonian Europe. Isaac Newton's famous "*hypotheses non fingo*" was a quip against the novel. A common put-down of a rival scientific theory in eighteenth-century France was "*mais ce n'est qu'un roman!*"

For the practices of reading, see Reinhard Wittmann, "Was There a Reading Revolution?," in *A History of Reading in the West*, ed. Guglielmo Cavallo and Roger Chartier (Amherst: University of Massachusetts Press, 1999), 284–312. A good example for the massive impact of epistolary novels is Denis Diderot's 1761 *Éloge de Richardson* (Paris: BnF, 2016). For the emergence of suspense as a narrative quality in the nineteenth century—culminating in the detective novel of the late nineteenth century—see Peter Brooks, *Reading for the Plot: Design and Intention in Narrative* (Cambridge, MA: Harvard University Press, 1984); for the English market, see Linda Hughes and Michael Lund, *The Victorian Serial* (Charlottesville: University of Virginia Press, 1991) and Louis James, *The Victorian Novel* (Malden, MA: Blackwell, 2006).

I apologize for the coinage seriability; it can only be justified by referring to the massive research and synthesizing argument that Clare

Pettitt makes in *Serial Forms: The Unfinished Project of Modernity, 1815–1848* (New York: Oxford University Press, 2020). With its even more comprehensive companion volume, *Serial Revolutions 1848: Writing, Politics, Form* (New York: Oxford University Press, 2022), she reconstructs and makes visible the network, the many conditions that sustain the novel in the nineteenth century. These conditions have their antecedents in the formal affordances of the novel.

For the relation of narrative and suspense, see Caroline Levine, *The Serious Pleasure of Suspense* (Charlottesville: University of Virginia Press, 2003). For the reciprocal experiences of novel and readers, the most clamorous case before industrial serialization was Laurence Sterne's *Tristram Shandy*, which appeared over a span of seven years and incorporated in its later volumes responses to criticism and allusions to recent events; see Alsop, *Practices of Reading*, 28–50. The prominence of Sam Weller in Dickens's *The Pickwick Papers* in response to sales figures is a later example. For the industrial conditions of nineteenth-century novels, see also my *The Cylinder: Kinematics of the Nineteenth Century* (Berkeley: University of California Press, 2012), 103–112.

For a richly illustrated account of the metaphysics of fictional worlds, see Thomas Pavel, *Fictional Worlds* (Cambridge, MA: Harvard University Press, 1984), esp. 114–135; the chapter is entitled, oblivious of Buddhist terminology, "Conventions." There have been various attempts to link the doctrine of two truths to philosophical fictionalism; see, for example, Mario d'Amato, "Buddhist Fictionalism," *Sophia* 52 (2013): 409–424, and Tom Tillemans, "How Far Can a Mādhyamika Buddhist Reform Conventional Truth? Dismal Relativism, Fictionalism, and Easy-Easy Truth, and the Alternatives," in *Moonshadows: Conventional Truth in Buddhist Philosophy*, ed. the Cowherds (Oxford: Oxford University Press, 2011), 151–165. Jay Garfield (in *The Fundamental Wisdom*) uses "reification" and "reificationist" as a collective noun for external and internal opponents of Nāgārjuna. For a more recent reconsideration of the concept (without reference to Buddhism), see Axel Honneth, *Reification: A New Look at an Old Idea* (Oxford: Oxford University Press, 2008).

Reading Experience III
Hélène Cixous, *1938, nuits*

I have been sent a lot of Hélène Cixous's novels, if that's the right
term for the autofictional narratives she has produced at a staggering clip since the late 1960s. I have met her, I love her as a
person, and many years ago, I even translated one of her books
from French into German. But I must confess that I find many
of her works, perhaps most of them, difficult to get into; her
French is difficult in the way French prose of the 1970s is
difficult—full of self-references, puns, allusions, repetitions, to
say nothing of the absence of characterizations, exposition, even
punctuation. I love looking at and handling the small Galilée
books with their French flap, their serif typeface, and that strang-
est and most French of all printing conventions, the "prière
d'insérer," an inserted abstract that does more to mystify than
spark a reader's interest. Typically, when I receive a book, I look
at it, leaf through it, and then lay it aside for a later time that
rarely comes. I did the same with *1938, nuits* (2019), but was suddenly captivated by the reproduction of two pages of a typescript in German. What was it?

Cixous's fiction has always circled around her family's history,
which is full of events that are all the more extraordinary because
they have at their center a protagonist who is resolutely, stub-
bornly ordinary: her mother Eva Klein, who died at the age of
103 in 2013. Born into a well-established Ashkenazi Jewish family
in Osnabrück, she left Germany for France even before the rise
of the Nazis, married the Sephardic radiologist Georges Cixous,

and moved with him to Oran in Algeria. Since his death in 1948 she has fended for herself and for her children first in Algeria and then, after Algerian independence, in Paris. She did not return to Osnabrück until the city invited her in the 1990s.

1938, nuits is about the pogroms against German Jews after the staged burning of the German parliament. Her mother's family in Osnabrück had been dismissive of the Nazi threat until the chaotic night of November 9, 1938, when the local synagogue burned down and the Jews of the town were rounded up, beaten, and taken to Buchenwald, the camp established just outside of Weimar, the city of Johann Wolfgang von Goethe, Franz Liszt, and Friedrich Nietzsche. The historical core of that story is documented by a young doctor called Siegfried (Fred)—a childhood friend of Eva's—who had come back to Osnabrück from his medical training in Basel and was swept up in the arrests and deported to Buchenwald; he was then released and emigrated to the United States where he wrote down his experiences and sent the manuscript, many years later, to Cixous's mother.

What had caught my eye were the two pages of Fred's typescript that are reproduced in the book. A doctor's clinical eye here records in German the humiliations to which the prisoners are subjected. Are there national differences in brutality? The petty rules, the emphasis on performative discipline, the hierarchy among the soldiers and guards feel terrifyingly familiar to me (I have served in the German *Bundeswehr*). Prisoners die, but the camps are not yet calibrated for the task of extermination, which gives the entire scenario the eerie and revolting feel of a dress rehearsal. I read every account of the Holocaust and the preparations for it with a mixture of trepidation, lurid eagerness, and a sensation of horror that comes from the deeply felt possibility of having been involved in it and not knowing on which side.

The peculiarities of Cixous's writing style that so often have irritated me—the difficulty of telling where and when an event takes place, who is speaking, her stopping to let a word roll off her writerly tongue or to focus on a minute detail as if it contained the key to all questions: suddenly they seem the only way to let the reader experience the chaos and the peculiar violence of this night. The most unsettling scenes in the novel are those that show how former friends, classmates, or customers turn away from their Jewish neighbors once the mass frenzy of the night of the ninth has given everyone license to let go of their *Anstand*, the decency Germans—until today!—claim is part of their national character. The incredulousness of the members of Eva's family is as shocking as the sudden turn to cruelty and coldness of their neighbors.

Once the frightened Jews are rounded up and held in enclosures for all to see, the word that dominates the texts for me is "deportation," present here in all the details that come with the forcible removal of thousands of human bodies through a country ostensibly not at war. The denunciations, the collaboration between police and railway administration, the passivity, or taunting aggression, of the bystanders, the frantic cruelty of the guards—Cixous makes these experiences unbearably vivid by putting her narrating voice in the holding cell, on the seat in the bus, on the ramp at Buchenwald, in the barracks. It is devastating to experience these scenes in the reading and having to imagine them as playing out in the past, in the present, and in the future, here and elsewhere.

The full horror of Fred's experiences thus becomes readable to me not in the sober descriptions of the document he himself wrote and sent to Cixous's mother (who promptly forgot about it) but in the contrastive embedding in Cixous's extravagant stylings. Either I have done her an injustice with my impatience with her previous work or this novel is the one in which her writing comes fully into its own.

I realize now what others have figured out long before me: that the reality of this experience reaches me and touches me because it is written as fiction, because this mode allows Cixous to break down the overwhelming solidity of historical facts into the hypergranularity of sensations—the smell of a newspaper, the furtive glance of a friend who has just betrayed us, the light in the barracks—that I recognize as a reaction to trauma. Fred's document, even though more "realistic," did not and could not have this effect.

And then there it is, one of these small miracles that can happen when the experience of the reader suddenly touches the experiences in the book: Fred, in search of a place to finish his medical studies, goes to Paris and is there, through acquaintances of acquaintances, introduced to another exiled German Jew with whom he has a long discussion about—experience (highlighted by Cixous through the German "Erfahrung"). The conversation was memorable enough for Fred to remember and recount it even late in his life. The interlocutor was Walter Benjamin.

Chapter 6 | **The Experience of Reading**

The perspective offered here—that the novel emerged from the strictures of theology and philosophy and harnessed the industrial epoch's technical possibilities to become the dominant medium of experience until the advent of film in the early twentieth century—restores agency and hence experience and singularity to the novel itself. For a comprehensive understanding of experience, the three philosophers we have consulted agree that the distinction between a human subject that has the experience and an inert object that is experienced is only a provisional construct to establish order in a fluid, intermingled relation. Many traditional histories of the novel tacitly acknowledge this fluidity when they talk about the "rise" or "theory" of the novel, toggling between subjective and objective readings of this genitive. On closer inspection, however, most narratives of the rise of the genre presuppose essentialist theories of development—the emergence of realistic modes of representation, for example, or the mutual influence between author and market—in which novels are not agents but cases.

Novels since the middle of the nineteenth century are realistic in the sense that they enter as serialized products the spatial and temporal field of the readers' experience—be this as successively released installments, as complete volumes, or both. Often, the publisher or the fame of the author creates a halo of expectation around them, further binding readers to "their" novel and author. By the time a novel reaches its readers, it has undergone a series of experiences itself. It has emerged from the author's lived experience (and its multiple conditions) and met with the demands of the publisher, who in turn has adapted to pressures of the market and the limits of technical reproduction and distribution. The adoption of free indirect discourse in the middle of the nineteenth century, to mention a feature that I will discuss later, is the result of an experience the novel *Madame Bovary* made in 1857 with the author, the publisher, the reading public, the courts, and the politics of the Second Empire. Books do not simply have their fate; like animals, landscapes, or rooms, they *are* experiences, which in turn intersect with the experiences of a reading human.

This change in perspective allows us to see the difference between aesthetic categories, like originality, and the notion of singularity that the radical empiricism of Nāgārjuna, Nietzsche, and William James entails. Originality inserts a stopgap into the multitude of causes and allocates unprecedented firstness either to an author or to a work; it is modeled after the creative power of the Christian God and forces reading into the position of posthumous exegesis. Singularity acknowledges that every work is infinitely conditioned and therefore exceeds the horizon of author and reader—it is novel in the empirical sense of the word.

This intersection of the experience of the novel and the experience of the reader is the experience of reading. Like narrative fiction itself, reading is a social and technical experience that has undergone, and is at present undergoing, dramatic changes. We are implicitly aware of this historicity when we worry, for example, that our students lose the experience of immersive reading, and with it their ability to acquire the empathy that comes from identifying and suffering with a fictional character, from inhabiting another's moral universe. It is this latter ability that is often mentioned when the question arises what it is that literary studies, in the most general sense, contribute to the undergraduate curriculum and to the pedagogical mission of colleges and universities. Reading literature, in particular literature not written in a reader's language, broadens their moral horizon and, more recently, furthers their cognitive flexibility.

This line of arguing for the value of immersive, imaginative reading is of venerable provenance, reaching back to the moral sense of Scripture, especially in its Protestant incarnation, which in turn was co-conditioned by the emergence of the printing press. The printed page—uniform and stripped of visual distractions— focused attention on a vanishing point beyond the text, where identification with the story's protagonist could play out within the reader's imagination. In the theology of Protestant and Pietist Bible study, reading became a relation of "influence," a channel through which the spirit could flow into the reader's soul. In this imaginary immediacy of absorption, writing—the activity as well as its technological manifestation in print—notoriously disappeared from the purview of literary interpretation.

The disruptive success of novels in the latter half of the eighteenth century owed much to authors' subtle exploitation of readers' willingness to be "influenced." The extreme emotional reactions of both male and female readers of Samuel Richardson (*Clarissa*, 1748) and Jean-Jacques Rousseau (*Julie; or, The New Heloise*, 1761) or male readers adopting Werther's yellow-and-blue outfit after the first publication of Johann Wolfgang von Goethe's *The Sufferings of Young Werther* (1774) illustrate how this biblical disposition migrated into the encounter with secular literature and overwhelmed the ironic distancing of the fictional editor. The epistolary novel, in particular, obliterated the distance between protagonist and readers, creating an intimacy so powerful that in the second edition of *The Sufferings of Young Werther* Goethe had to exhort his readers not to follow the model of the poor suicide.

Against the attraction of tropological "lay" reading that began in the late eighteenth century (though Miguel de Cervantes had diagnosed its pitfalls much earlier), academic literary scholarship and teaching bundled the remaining three senses into stages of interpretation that each still have prominent support and occasion methodological debate. The literal sense, we have seen, merged with the practices of classical philology and helped establish a science of "objective" editing, historical explanation, and, more recently, materialist speculation. Allegorical readings became the domain of scholars who investigate the anxiety of influence literary texts exert on each other, often across the entire continuum of the Western tradition. The last decades of the twentieth century saw the rise of readings that focused on allegorical relations within single works, relations that would subvert their claims to wholeness of meaning. Contemporary anagogical readings are those that situate literary works against the background of historical and political developments, most often against the logic and crises of late capitalism.

Despite their claims to perform "readings," contemporary exegetes of secular literature rarely consider reading as an embodied experience. Research in the physiology, psychology, and sociology of reading seldom informs literary studies, where "reading" is taken as a synonym for performing critical and distanced analyses on literary texts. Even the formerly accepted task of interpretation—to attempt answers to the question of what a work of literature might mean for the reader, for the author, or for a community—from the impersonal perspective of such "readings" appears as too immersed in individuality and divination.

Yet it is in this pursuit of scientific objectivity that the metaphysical burden of reading comes to the fore: "reading" attempts to "save the phenomena" by converting materiality into ideality, by elevating an aggregate (of letters) into a unity (of meaning), into the totality of a "work," even if critical readings often show that this totality is illusory. The Greek etymology conjoining reading, gathering, and reason, *legein* and *logos*, further strengthened this metaphysical bond.

When Christianity transitioned from an apocalyptic movement to a religion of the book, it developed exegetical strategies that, for thousands of years, provided readers with keys to the infinite riches of Scripture. But these strategies—codified in the quadruple sense of the Scriptures—were originally secular and had their origin in Alexandrine and Roman philology; they did not provide a theological account for the mystery of reading as the human encounter with the divine word. As reading Scripture became increasingly central to understanding God's revelation, it merged with the growing devotion to the mystery of Incarnation—the Word made flesh.

The primal scene of Christian reading is depicted in the countless images of the Annunciation and replicated in modernity in the many depictions of absorbed (and therefore vulnerable) female readers. In most images since the early Renaissance, the Virgin Mary is shown seated alone, typically in an enclosed room or garden, reading a passage of the Old Testament that Christian iconology has identified as Isaiah 7:14: "Therefore the Lord himself will give you a sign: the virgin will conceive and give birth to a son, and will call him Immanuel." It is at this moment of absorption that the angel of the Annunciation swoops in—in early medieval versions often bearing a text of his own, the Ave that proclaims Mary as already full of the grace whose incarnation she will bring to term.

Without the angel's intervention, Mary would have "known" what she was reading; she would have captured the literal sense of the passage in Isaiah but could not have understood its spiritual meaning—its typological relation to the yet-to-be-written New Testament, its meaning for her own life, and its meaning for the history of salvation, which takes such a dramatic turn with this announcement. In the language of Saint Paul, the letter was dead to her until the angel vivified it.

Mary's full comprehension of her reading is a miracle—a transformation and transubstantiation of words read and spoken into the understanding of their meaning and the incarnation of this comprehension in the body of her son, Jesus. The scene of the Annunciation—conflated pictorially and calendrically with the act of Conception—aligns reading and conceiving; it gives us a glimpse of reading as an embodying and embodied experience, even if the Dogma goes to spectacular lengths to erase the ink spot, the *macula*, that would have betrayed the enjambment of body and spirit, of *legein* and *logos*.

There is, then, buried in this focal scene of Christianity the recognition that reading is a genuine embodied experience, and that in this embodiment it is open to a wholly novel, as yet incomprehensible future; it figures as miraculous the moment in which self and other touch and change before separating again into the stark dichotomies required by the metaphysics of the Word. William James describes and normalizes this miracle, this fusion and flux, as "pure experience"—a miracle to which we have become oblivious under the incessant pressure to separate, judge, and opine.

At the end of his life, the savior thus conceived also requires an act of reading and transubstantiation from his disciples. He is asking, however, for a reversal of incarnation, for the transformation of objects of the outer world into symbols of faith. The Institution of the Eucharist is the antitype to the Annunciation: declaring wine to be his blood and bread to be his body, Jesus asks his apostles to dis-incarnate objects, to read them into their memory and to hold fast to this transformation by repeating, by instantiating it. Whereas the angel asks Mary to believe in the future, Jesus asks the apostles to believe in the past and thus for their willingness to recognize things as signs, to interpret.

This paradigm, in which reading is conceived as an act of faith and interpretation as a work of commemoration, as the constant shuttling between symbolization and literalization, has weighed heavily on Western conceptions of reading. Secular and academic practices of literary interpretation have found it difficult to fully shed this weight. Reading is still seen—at least in the academic humanities—as an activity fundamentally different from other practices that help us navigate through life, like drawing, cycling, or cooking. When "lay" reading became exponentially more extensive in the nineteenth century, professional readers in the academy retained, even increased, their focus on the depth and meticulousness of their retroactive reading. The Marian dimension of hope and radical change through reading has been overwhelmed by the apostolic work of interpretating signs and symbols. Most importantly, reading remains enclosed in subjectivity.

A complementary legacy of our apostolic reading is the assumption that a text's meaning is already "there," independent of a reader's engagement with it. This conviction is most strikingly institutionalized in the Catholic Church's Index Librorum Prohibitorum, in the restricted-access collections in national libraries—the Enfer in the French National Library, the Private Case in the British Library—and in contemporary censorship indices from Florida to Alabama. At first glance, sequestering books may seem like a reasonable if antiquated and restrictive policy, but it bears reflecting upon its underlying assumption that a set of nonpictorial marks elicit the same mental reaction in all members of a language community. It is a vivid example of why Nāgārjuna insists on the reality of conventional truth; it shows how stable our conventions—the conventions that make up our languages, decency laws, social narratives, political arguments—are even though they lack any permanent, mind-independent essence.

James's radical empiricism offers a pathway to liberate reading from its recognitive and subjective constraints, to rewild it into a genuine—open, mutual, nonconceptual—experience. He had determined—in his empirical work with patients as well as in his survey of religious experiences—that in their "pure," inarticulate state, human experiences are infinitely variegated and infinitely connected. They are not isolated, separate, sequential events but continuously intermixed with subtler experiences that we, having only so much attention to allocate, suppress in the busy flow of day-to-day life. Though James does not himself make the connection, we can see in this infinite web of experiences an avatar of Nāgārjuna's *pratītyasamutpāda*—the web of infinite conditions that relates phenomena to their proximate causes and empties them of substantial identity.

James articulates in Western terms the implications of thinking through the absolute priority of experience. First is the unseating of the preexisting, consciousness-endowed human subject that has the experience; second the attribution of experience to things typically regarded as inanimate or unconscious. What philosophy ambiguously designates as "subject" and "object" are, for James, just termini of a particular sequence of experiences—one is equipped with the means to mentally reflect on experiences, the other is slower and physical in its reactions. When a human subject claims sole ownership of its experiences, it dismisses the experiential potential of all other elements in the web of conditions. The epistemological, social, and ecological consequences of this degradation have often been chronicled.

Consider a hike in the foothills. A rationalist might describe it as the movement of human "thinking things" through a non-thinking, more or less inert landscape, undertaken for the—articulated or recoverable—purpose of exercising, contemplating, or doing research, at the end of which the humans can reflect on the activity and commit it to internal or externalized memory. In James's experience-centered view, by contrast, the same event is the experience named "hiking" that connects human individuals in motion with an environment that is equally, albeit more slowly, in motion. The hikers have behind them a series of experiences that led them to the hike, and ahead of them experiences in which the hike will be a smaller or larger factor. But the landscape also has a long series of geological and botanical experiences behind it, and it, too, will carry the memory of its experience with the hikers and reflect on it by changing and adapting—for example, by trail erosion on a local, or by climate change on a global scale. Object and subject, passivity and activity, are only the most abstract, barren termini on a sliding scale of entanglement, not entities that are given before the experience commences or after it ends.

It is the same with reading. Rather than seeing it as the activity of a solitary subject who picks up an inert object—a book or a tablet—and transubstantiates its dead letters into thoughts and spiritual meaning, it can be more richly described as the intersection of two experiential lines: one is constituted by the experiences of the reader—by her personal history, her current state of mind, her motivation for picking up this particular book, the location where she is doing the reading, her hopes for the future, even her neuronal pathways, among other things; the other line is constituted by the experiences of the book—by its own emergence from the intersection of authorial intentions, genre conventions, and market pressures, by its inclusion into various streams of recommendations and canonizations, including college syllabi, and by the affordances of its layout, type, and size. The fulcrum of this intersection is the experience of the characters, in both senses of the genitive: the experiences the characters make and thus turn this book into a novel, and the experience the reader makes with the character, on which the next chapter will concentrate.

Recent research in the history of the book as the medium of modernity reinforces this shift away from understanding reading as a one-sided activity. Through design, type, title, chapter length, format, price, and seasonal book fairs, novels in the eighteenth century lured ever more readers into their world; when serialization became the standard for success in the nineteenth century, this reciprocity of reading and being read reached new heights—the famous cliffhanger at the end of an installment, the insertion of characters that "polled well," the tailoring of narratives to the time and attention spans of railway travelers, the reviews and book clubs that debated novels during their print run, and the spectacular obscenity trials in the 1850s. All of these developments testify to a reciprocal flow of energy between book and reader that belies the idea that reading is a silent, secluded, immersive theater of the mind.

Experimental physiology of the mid-nineteenth century, with which James was intimately familiar, found that reading eyes jump in saccades, in rapid, jerky movements backward and forward that knit together the text rather than scan it in one continuous motion. There is no physiological equivalent to the focused intent to understand and the gradual decipherment of meaning as which reading is so often conceived. The eye in its forward movement seems to fight the resistance of print and grammar by advancing and retreating, incorporating new information by comparing it to what is already known. Everybody who has had the misfortune of having to learn German knows how in a long sentence the eye desperately lurches to the end to find the verb that gives meaning to what comes before. At this microscopic range—the eye apparently makes these jumps five times per second—reading exhibits the same characteristics as all experiences: a constant, ungrounded back-and-forth between activity and passivity, between what only later we call reader and book, subject and object.

In its deep entanglement with its "object," reading is an experience not essentially different from other forms of experiences. If we seek to analyze it with a focus on scientifically quantifiable knowledge, we can investigate the subjective terminus and go back all the way to the neurological and optical processes that transform light contrast—black type on white paper—into words, sentences, and narratives. Alternatively, we can concentrate on the objective terminus and look at the book, its history, its kinematics, its design. Just as there is no single point in the growth of an embryo where we say, "Now it is a human being," there is no point in the relation between reader and book where the transubstantiation from letter into spirit palpably occurs. The closer we look at it, the "purer" the experience of reading becomes—pure in James's sense that under attentive inspection our experiences dissolve into preconceptual "droplets" of experience that contain their conventional termini (in this case reader and text) in an undifferentiated state of potential.

Reading is a paradigmatic case for the artificial problems that dualistic theological, cognitive, and epistemological approaches to experience generate. So long as we think of reading solely as divination, as decoding, or as a cultural technique, we presuppose the very duality that we later fail to overcome. We strip an experience of its temporal and incremental unfolding, of its back-and-forth of reading on and reflecting back and instead seek to capture it with atemporal concepts. "Causality" then reemerges as the construct that must link two distinct poles or phases of what is one experience. Since by definition we can neither observe nor deduce causality, we grasp at higher-order, transcendental guarantees that give coherence to our explanations. Once embarked on this road of causal explanations, we divide the temporal continuity of an experience into near-spatial packages of before and after that we must relate again by concepts or categories. Yet as James has pointed out, causality is only the most abstract end point of a multitude of relations that precede or coexist with it, such as simultaneity and time interval, space adjacency, resistance, similarity, and reciprocity.

We should not fear a gap in our understanding of the world if we resist the reduction of experiences like reading to abstract causal chains with determinate beginning and end points. Of course, as clinicians or educators we may want to understand why some people have greater difficulties reading than others, or why some media are more conducive to immersive reading than others, and for such purposes we may want to resort to the causal reasoning of the physical and historical sciences. But if this causal chain cannot be stretched across the entire expanse of the reading experience, so be it. We are constantly involved in experiences that are, though intimate and manifest, causally inexplicable. Think of being in love.

Bringing James's radical empiricism to bear on the history and practice of reading frees it from the enclosure in subjectivity and aligns it with other experiences. This normalization of reading at the same time sheds a light back on experience: in its temporal unfolding, its proceeding in jumps back and forth, experience has the form of reading, a fact we acknowledge in such locutions as "reading a situation" or "reading a room."

It is in this congruity of reading and experiencing that the true value of speaking and writing about reading literature within and outside of academia lies. If reading is a paradigmatic case of experiencing, then getting students and readers to attend to this experience, getting them to articulate and reflect on it, has a propaedeutic function for a more compassionate attitude to their own experiences as well as toward those of others.

Bibliographical Essay

One of the insights in Dominick LaCapra's meticulous reconstruction in *"Madame Bovary" on Trial* (Ithaca, NY: Cornell University Press, 1986) is that it really was the novel that was on trial; such was the effectiveness of free indirect discourse that neither publisher nor author could be linked to the novel beyond reasonable doubt. The most eloquent proponent for the moral benefits of reading novels is still Martha Nussbaum in *Love's Knowledge: Essays on Philosophy and Literature* (Oxford: Oxford University Press, 1990). This suppression of writing was, of course, the starting point for Jacques Derrida's investigations in *Of Grammatology* (Baltimore: Johns Hopkins University Press, 1998). The more technical arguments about the relation between the barrenness of the printed page and the excitement of the imagination were made by Walter J. Ong in *Orality and Literacy* (London: Routledge, 2012) and, more flamboyantly still, by Friedrich Kittler in *Discourse Networks 1800/1900* (Stanford, CA: Stanford University Press, 1992). For the career of "influence" as an astrological, religious, and philosophical concept, see Rainer Specht, "Einfluß," in *Historisches Wörterbuch der Philosophie* (Basel: Schwabe, 2017).

A most startling document of the impact of Richardson's novels is the *Éloge de Richardson* (1761) by the usually clearheaded Denis Diderot (Paris: BnF, 2016). Goethe put a warning to the readers of his *Die Leiden des jungen Werthers*—"be a man, do not follow him"—into the second edition (Leipzig: Weygand, 1775) after he heard reports that there were copycat suicides. For the transformation of moral-focused sacred reading to lay reading, see Roger Chartier, "Du Livre au Lire," in *Sociologie de la Communication*, ed. Paul Beaud (Paris: Presses Universitaires de France, 1977), 271–290. A glorious counterexample to this neglect of corporeal reading is Nicholas Dames, *The Physiology of the Novel: Reading, Neural Science, and the Form of Victorian Fiction* (Oxford: Oxford University Press, 2007). Dames seeks to recover the outlines of a Victorian science of reading that in turn shaped the form of nineteenth-century novels (the length of installments, the shape of chapters, the number of characters).

For the science and history of reading, I have consulted Adrian Johns, *The Science of Reading* (Chicago: University of Chicago Press, 2023); Maryanne Wolf, *Proust and the Squid: The Story and Science of the Reading Brain* (New York: Harper, 2008); Shafquat Towheed, Rosalind Crone, and Katie Hasley, eds., *The History of Reading* (London: Routledge, 2010); Stanislas Dehaene, *Reading in the Brain: The New Science of How We Read* (New York: Penguin, 2010), which beautifully compares the emergence of meaning to a tidal bore, 113–115; Alexander Honold and Rolf Pfarr, eds., *Grundthemen der Literaturwissenschaft: Lesen* (Berlin: de Gruyter, 2018); Julika Griem, *Szenen des Lesens: Schauplätze einer gesellschaftlichen Selbstverständigung* (Bielefeld: transcript, 2021); and Ingo Berensmeyer, *A Short Media History of English Literature* (Berlin: de Gruyter, 2022). For the theology and iconography of the Annunciation, see Sarah Drummond, *Divine Conception: The Art of the Annunciation* (London: Unicorn, 2018) and Laura Saetveit Miles, "The Origins and Development of the Virgin Mary's Book at the Annunciation," *Speculum* 89, no. 3 (July 2014): 632–669. For the relation of conventional truth, language, and institutions of meaning, see Jan Westerhoff, "The Merely Conventional Existence of the World," in *Moonshadows: Conventional Truth in Buddhist Philosophy*, ed. the Cowherds (Oxford: Oxford University Press, 2011), 189–212.

James's harshest criticism of subjectivity as the originator of experience is in "Does 'Consciousness' Exist?," in *Writings, 1902–1910* (New York: Library of America, 1988), 1141–1158. The degradation of the object is probably the area where James and Martin Heidegger (who, like Edmund Husserl, had read James) would agree most. The thought experiment of the hike is inspired by Bruno Latour, who in his *An Inquiry into Modes of Existence* (Cambridge, MA: Harvard University Press, 2013) recounts the conditioned arising of an Alpine hiking path (74–77). Latour was an unequivocal if clandestine admirer of James: "Let us recall that radical empiricism, the version that inspired William James and that this entire inquiry aspires to extend in a more systematic way, reconnects the thread of experience by attaching prepositions to what follows them, to what they merely announce, utter, dispatch. To follow experience, for second-wave empiricism, is thus to follow—by a leap, a hiatus, a mini-transcendence—the movement for a preposition to what it indicates, prepares for, or *designates*" (Latour, *Inquiry*, 236). For recent research in the activity of the text in making us read, see Multigraph Collective, *Interacting with Print: Elements of Reading in the Era of Print*

Saturation (Chicago: University of Chicago Press, 2017) and Carlos Spoerhase, *Das Format der Literatur: Praktiken materieller Textualität zwischen 1740 und 1830* (Göttingen: Wallstein, 2018).

James describes the two directions of inquiry thusly: "A sensible 'experience' of mine, say this book written on by this pen, leads in one dimension into the world of matter, paper-mills, etc., in the other into that psychologic life of mine of which it is an affection. Both sets of associates are contiguous with it, yet one set must be dropped out of sight if the other is to be followed. They decline to make one universe in the absolute sense of something that can be embraced by one individual stroke of apprehension" (*Notebook J*, William James Papers, Houghton Library, Harvard University, bMS Am 1092.9 [4509]).

For saccades in eye movement, see Dehaene, *Reading in the Brain*, 13–18. For the notion of droplets of experience (*Erfahrungströpfchen*), see the excellent reconstruction in Felicitas Krämer, *Erfahrungsvielfalt und Wirklichkeit: Zu William James' Realitätsverständnis* (Göttingen: Vandenhoeck & Ruprecht, 2006), 143–212. For the prepositions that antecede "because," see William James, "A World of Pure Experience," in *Writings, 1902–1910* (New York: Library of America, 1987), 1161.

Reading Experience IV
Heinrich von Kleist, *Die Marquise von O . . .*

Without thinking too much about it, I assigned Heinrich von Kleist's 1808 novella *The Marquise of O . . .* for a senior seminar on German short stories. It seemed the right length, and I remembered that on a previous occasion, many years ago, discussion in class had been quite lively. Another convenience of the text is that it allows teachers to demonstrate to students the continued powers of exegetical readings—in particular, the *sensus historicus* by pointing to the emergence of newspapers as new media of mass communication at the beginning of the nineteenth century, and the *sensus allegoricus* by drawing the parallels between the announcement in the newspaper posted by the Marquise and the Annunciation to the Virgin Mary, the scene that is so deeply woven into the Western metaphysics of reading, transubstantiation, and reproduction.

To briefly summarize the story: in the turmoil of a military assault on the fortress defended by her father's troops, a young, widowed Marquise tries to flee the assailants but faints. A few months later she finds herself pregnant. Steadfastly insisting on her chastity and abandoned by her family, she finally puts an advertisement in the local newspaper asking for the father to come forward at a specified time and place, promising to marry him. Meanwhile, a Russian officer who had been her protector during the assault returns and asks for her hand, which she refuses until the father of her child is found. On the appointed day the Russian officer reveals himself as her rapist. The Marquise is at first horrified but later relents and confesses that she had loved him since she first laid eyes on him.

As is not usual in my field, the seminar of seven students consisted entirely of young women. Their grasp of German was good, in two instances excellent. We began with a discussion of Kleist's style, his extreme density and hypotaxis that to students read almost like a caricature of the German we had trained them to speak. I then asked them to summarize the story—my plan was to introduce the distinction between story and plot and then to talk about censorship around 1800. Two of the women said that they had tried to figure out the story together but couldn't. It wasn't a question of vocabulary. What they got was a story of a rape that detailed the shaming and abandonment of the victim and then ended with the marriage between rapist and victim. Surely, that couldn't be right?

I had begun working on the present project at the time but had somehow not considered what it would mean for my teaching of texts that, like Kleist's, have the potential to retraumatize students, or at least force them into a conversation that they might find uncomfortable. I knew that sexual assault, and perhaps even rape, was within the ambit of my students' experiences on campus; I have also argued that we have no access to others' experiences—can never "share" them—and therefore cannot even estimate how upsetting it might be to read about them or discuss them in class, in this case with a male teacher.

It is not a question of condemning Kleist for writing a story about rape; though in other stories he shows a worrying penchant for graphic violence, rape, in connection with middle-class rejection of aristocratic immorality, was a constant topic in the literature of the late eighteenth century, most famously perhaps in Samuel Richardson's immensely popular *Clarissa*. I can give this background to the students; I can point to the artfulness with which Kleist avoids representing the rape and keeps even the main characters in the novella guessing. But no amount of exegetical labor can deny the "thatness" of my students' experience, and its invisibility to me. The experiential approach to the reading of prose fiction claims to reach into the reality of a reader's life—this is a case where this claim must draw consequences.

During my training in the late '80s and early '90s, Kleist was a favorite because he could serve as a counterfigure to the Goethe establishment without, however, rocking the foundation of the discipline, and because his prose and his dramatic imagination are at times so extreme that they offer themselves to close, deconstructive readings. Such readings, by implication, would disregard all "soft," affective dimensions and try to dissolve the propositional and narrative surface of a text into its constitutive, counterintuitive, often incompatible elements. The famous dash which Kleist puts in place of a verbal representation of the rape has given rise to a voluminous literature on the theory of literary representation.

From the perspective here proposed, from which the experiential involvement of the reader in the reading is of paramount importance—especially of young, "uncritical," "lay" readers—the abstraction from the affective dimension is not possible. Yet canceling Kleist or similar authors for undergraduate courses is equally absurd, if only because that would require abstract rules of selection that an empiricist approach cannot supply. This is a case where it helps to remember the pragmatic roots of radical empiricism. I can make the determination for myself that I will not teach this text to undergraduates without requiring the same from my colleagues who might be better prepared, better positioned, or more fearless than I am. The downside of my decision is minimal—there are plenty of other texts, even by Kleist, that I can teach instead. It is hard to take seriously the objection that a student's education, or even their knowledge of German literature, would be compromised if they never read Kleist's *Marquise of O . . .*

Chapter 7 | Reading Experiences

The previous two chapters have explored the novel experience from two different sides: the first focused on the novel as a convention that, in the modern West, became the dominant form for articulating the vagaries of human experiences. It achieved this dominance by developing a rich network of conditions that reach from the kinematics of industrial machines to narratological innovations that make the reading of experience possible and desirable. In a different register, this is the side of the object, though the analysis given here has tried to show that such rigid designations fail—is the character in a novel an object?—and that novels should be understood as concretized, singular experiences. The last chapter looked at the novel experience from the side of the "subject," the reader who intersects with the novel in the experience of reading; it urged a broadening of our understanding of reading from the notion of univocal deciphering to recognizing it as a temporally extended embodied practice in which the poles of activity and passivity remain fluid, thus aligning it with the general view of experience this essay proposes.

The following pages attempt to get closer to the multiple conditions that render the reading of experiences in a novel an avatar of experience as such. The first step on this approach is the observation that experiences in their "pure" state—in their incessant shuttling between subjective and objective termini—have no inherent form, but that the accounts we give of our experiences almost always have the structure of narratives, complete with a subject as the "owner" of the experience, obstacles that seem to oppose the intent of that subject, a beginning, middle, and end, and some continuous development between them. We tend to think of our experiences not so much as novel but as a novel.

At times—as children, as patients in therapy, or as students of meditation—we are urged to give up the impulse to turn our experiences into narratives, let go of the stories that position us as the heroes or, more often, the victims of conditions that we either overcome or that conspire against us. Friends or therapists try to convince us that our reading of a situation is far too egocentric, but letting go of the comforts of narratives is hard to do. They are our daily attempts "to save the phenomena": giving them a place in a story the outlines of which seem to be written not by but for us. There is, not incidentally, a great deal of ruminating by characters in modern novels themselves over the correlation of fate and contingency, and whether real novelty can even be narrated. Friedrich Nietzsche has shown that the hard and soft infrastructures of our world—institutions, social relations, artworks, universities—are themselves based on or built around narratives. The first chapter of this book highlighted how even the question of how to conceive of the world has been answered in the West with powerful narratives, beginning with Plato's demiurge and the Christian story of creation and draining into the Enlightenment idea of progress or Georg Wilhelm Friedrich Hegel's and Karl Marx's logic of history.

Under these auspices it is immensely difficult to disengage experiences from narrative form, to think of, for example, the beginning of an experience as not pregnant with its end, to distinguish proximity of conditions from causality, to think of an ending as a point in time rather than as a culmination. The three philosophers of experience we have interrogated, each in his own way and for his own reasons, have tried to untether experience from the grounding logic, the repetitiveness, and the predictability of narrative form even when they acknowledged its day-to-day utility. Their thinking of experience in this respect was literal: they urge us to gain a position outside of the established conventions to let us see our stories *as* stories.

It is no accident that the modern novel from its very beginning—in the startling composition that is *Don Quixote*—is fascinated by this difference in amplitude between the story in which the protagonist lives and the story the author gives us to read. When the knight of the woeful countenance charges the windmills, we as readers know that he mistakes preindustrial machines for monsters because he has subjected his experience entirely to the narratives he has consumed. We know this because of the form the modern novel begins to take here: the fictitious editor lets us see how, and even why, the protagonist mistakes his experiences for those in medieval narratives. These formal devices and their later descendants—the omniscient narrator and free indirect discourse—are, to repeat, not accidental to the novel but its innermost possibility.

Here already we can see that the distinction between the "truth" of a story and the narrative "illusion" capturing the characters in them, the distinction, ultimately, between a "pure" experience and its narrative capture, is not at all clear-cut. Not only is the world of the novel the result of multiple authorial choices but the actions of the characters are also, from a point of view we as critical and historically informed readers can occupy, often quite accurate in their illusoriness. Don Quixote correctly anticipates Marx's description of industrial, rotating machines as monsters, Emma Bovary's analyses of provincial life are not wrong; it is just that they cannot relate to their narratives *as* narratives.

There are some themes that for complex historical and social reasons lent themselves to novelistic narration—love, adultery, and ambition, to name the triad that dominates the Western canon—but it is more comprehensive still to say that novels in the West are particularly concerned with showing (and telling) the difference between how protagonists motivate and explain their behavior and the possible explanations the narrative frame allows us readers to arrive at. Often, this is the source of what we perceive as authorial irony, but it is much more than just a stylistic trait. Werther mistaking his envy for love, David

Copperfield admiring James Steerforth, Isabel Archer marrying Osmond—we read these disastrous developments with a parallax view that allows us both to see the power self-concocted narratives hold over a character and to anticipate their inevitable failure in the world created by the novel. The discrepancy between the protagonists' immersion in what they believe is the story of their experiences and the readers' appreciation of the wider circumstances in which this story loses its inevitability is a rudimentary source of suspense. To call the novel the medium of experience in modernity entails that it present experiences *as* narratives and allow for the precariousness of this relation to be experienced by the reader.

There is little doubt that novels since antiquity play on the reader's mimetic desires and on the pleasure of putting oneself into the position of a narrative's protagonist. Focusing on the tension between experience and narrative does not mean to deny these pleasures but to dispute their primacy. The previous chapter proposed the attribute "deep" for this focus, without attaching any value to this spatial metaphor. The idea of such reading is to hold open, at least tentatively and as a first step, the tension rather than to evaluate the resolution. William James had tried to advocate for a similar openness of experience when he reversed the order of feeling and emotions: just as emotions judge feelings and put themselves in their place, so do empathy and mimetic projection judge experience in lieu of appreciating its imperfection.

The difference between experience and its telling, we must remember, cannot be construed as that between two unrelated "essential" poles—between a pristine experience that is subsequently denatured by the demands of narrative—but as the constant shaping and reshaping of one by the other. Though fictional characters often yearn for an experience unspoiled by their present, "adult" narrative needs—a childhood memory, or a future ideal—modern, and especially realist, novels quite pitilessly show how every new, seemingly pristine and singular experience is already shaped by the conditions that surround it.

Novels of ambition often have the protagonist act consciously with a view to how an experience can be narrated. This relation between experience and its narrative uptake is an avatar of the distinction theories of the novel make between story (the linear unfolding of events) and plot (the modes of telling). Like that relation, it has both the advantage of suggesting momentary analytic clarity—here the story (experience), there the author's way of telling it (narration)—and the disadvantage of revealing that this difference cannot really be sustained.

Just as we cannot conceive of a story that has no plot-like arrangements or, inversely, of a pure arrangement without a story—though modernist writers like Ernest Hemingway or Samuel Beckett have certainly tried—there is no experience so pure that it is untouched by the circumstances in which it emerges. In Nāgārjuna's parlance, experiences do not have an essence, *svabhāva*, that would render them independent of their conditions. James's "pure experience" was always a clinical and speculative construct to help his argument for the valence of experience before its articulation and conceptualization.

This is, then, a first pedagogical fruit of the experiential approach to narrative literature: to train and sensitize a reader's awareness of the discrepancy between a character's conviction of the unconditionality, the individuality of their experiences and the inevitable discovery that they have conditionally arisen. For the novel of the late eighteenth and the nineteenth centuries—the form of which still dominates today's narrative culture—we can describe this discrepancy as the difference between characters believing that they are subjects of their experiences, that they *have* their experiences, and the slow or sudden realization that they *are* subject *to* their experiences, that experiences shape them.

In the German tradition, which significantly shaped European and North American narrative culture, the process of adjusting the presumptions of the individual to the "ways of the world" was, and is, called *Bildung*, the notoriously multivalent notion that, just like its relative "organic" that we encountered in the first chapter, suggested that natural and cultural processes of development are conjoined. As Hegel remarked, despite its invocation of growth and natural harmony, the bildungsroman of the nineteenth century was mostly a novel of disappointment and resignation. The experiential point of view here proposed gives Hegel's nostalgic assessment a more neutral color: its mournfulness would be justified only if one clings to the ideal of subjective ownership of experiences and to the idea of a meaningful world into which this subject may fit. If we release this nostalgia, what the novel allows us to read is another's experience—its conditioned development, its drama and pleasures, and, most fundamentally, what James calls its "thatness." The conflict between the striving of the individual and the resistance of the world is not *one* experience, it *is* experience. This realization, afforded by the novel, opens the reading of experiences in novels to the experience that is reading a novel, and ultimately to the awareness of our own experiences.

In the history of the novel, the tension between a character's self-understanding and the reader's view on their motivations, weaknesses, and strengths was initially marked by heavy authorial irony or by obvious signs to show the reader right from wrong. As the fictional editor merged into the omniscient narrator, this heavy-handedness also disappeared. Not only did the permeability of modern society make the distinction between right and wrong less obvious but also a new way of writing no longer required such judgment.

Free indirect discourse's ubiquitous use since the middle of the nineteenth century signals the emergence of a grammatical mood no longer associated with an actual, or even a possible, speaker position; it is plausible only within the development of the genre. The collapse of description into narration, of interior and exterior viewpoint—to briefly describe this new mood— does not extinguish the possibility of understanding an experience but complicates, and often suspends, the question of agency and moral significance. Insofar as experience in the full sense here uncovered also precedes the distinction of activity and passivity, of the subject and its antagonists, free indirect discourse, by holding these dichotomies in suspense, is experience's own language.

In the old regime of "pseudofactual" representation—in the found manuscript, the discovered epistolary, the unearthed diary—we encounter experiences either from the outside, as they are happening to the protagonist, or, in the case of the epistolary novels of the late eighteenth century, only from the inside (engendering the oft-noted problem of how to complete the narrative). In the "unspeakable" language of the omniscient narrator, by contrast, we read about experience from the outside, as other characters confront and engage with them, *and* from the inside, as a character ruminates, evaluates, and acts in them. The temporality of omniscient narration and the constant and inadvertent change of perspective in free indirect speech obliterate the distinction between inside and outside, between a subject that has the experience and a set of events that constrain it. In this innovative mode of narration, the modern novel thus finds a language that invites readers into regions of experiencing that have not yet congealed into separate, interpretable chunks.

This oscillation, which the French courts in Gustave Flaubert's and Charles Baudelaire's obscenity trials of 1857 so desperately wanted to arrest, does not simply represent experience in its state of constant change; it *is* that state. It asks the reader to stay alert and to sort through the many conditions that may influence and compose an event. Reading this strange, utterly unrealistic, inhuman voice, in which the separation between agent and action, purpose and obstruction, self and other must be supplied by the reader, is the moment in which reading about experience and the reading experience become one experience, become one with experience.

This is not to say that novels that do not employ free indirect discourse fall somehow short of the full potential of the genre. As a technical achievement, it is perhaps best compared with the invention of linear perspective—its absence in medieval or in cubist paintings does not detract from their value, but we post-

Renaissance viewers and readers carry this absence with us and often use it to gain clarity of a particular aspect of the work.

We may doubt whether novelistic literature allows for the genuine expression of experience and whether, by reacting to it as an experience, we are not chasing chimeras. Yet this is a worry only if we read for knowledge and truth. We need not go as far as Buddhist fictionalism and declare the difference between true and fictional manifestations of experience to be naught; it is enough to say that by entering the language game called novel, we accept it as an expression of another's experience, the truth of which we can never ascertain and anyway does not detract from, or add to, the reality of our experience reading it.

In the mutuality of the reading experience readers seek to make sense of a narrative and are themselves changed in the process. The minimal (but real) manifestation of that change is the temporal difference of having read a novel—a whole host of assumptions and expectations result from my having read, for example, *Invisible Man*, regardless of what I make of it. More likely, though, readers will relate the experiences they read about to the way they have, or would have, reacted in these or similar circumstances.

This need not lead to a conscious change in behavior—we may still become jealous even though we have read *Swann in Love*—but it opens a crack in the solidity of habit and repetition; it allows readers to disengage from their experiences and challenge their inevitability. After all, the otherness of experience not only pertains to another's experience but also to our own. In the process of reading, the fatality of our own experiences loosens up in the relative safety of a fictional narrative. At any moment, a novel's character could have acted otherwise; at any moment, we can act otherwise; at any moment, a novel may have a different impact on us. We can experience this loosening in other circumstances—hearing or practicing a piece of music, in a therapeutic setting, meeting someone—but during reading, as a spatial and temporally extended activity, we can reflect on it in the process. Reading novels takes time—time in which to reflect—because novels recount experiences that took time to make. In this equation lies the basis for any realism the novel may have.

While our daily experiences are constantly overlapping and, to a great extent, submerged under the habits we form and the conventions forced upon us, experiencing artworks often has a memorable beginning and end, and thus affords us the opportunity to reflect on an experience as singular. The moment when the houselights go down, when we enter a gallery space, or when we pick up a book marks the beginning of an experience that has corresponding marks at its end, when we leave the show, exit the gallery, put down the book. This is not to say that there are no antecedents or consequences that lead to and from these events, but—to take the case of reading a novel—the point where the life of the narrative and the life of the reader intersect is singular and often remains for the reader a distinct and memorable event.

This singularity reinforces the fact that other's experiences for us only have an outside. As R. D. Laing said, "I cannot experience your experience. You cannot experience my experience. We are both invisible men. All men are invisible to one another." We are, however, readable to one another. We practice this reading—in the full sense of the experience of reading, as developed above—when we seek to read how others experience. One way of doing this is to seek to read other's behavior as an expression of the sense they have made of their experiences. Another is to read novels—for example, *Invisible Man*. Readers will still not experience what the narrator recounts. They will not experience what a Black man in the 1930s and '40s experienced. But this "not" is not nothing; this impossibility is itself an experience, the experience of the otherness of someone's experience.

Yet another way is to open a conversation about the experience of reading. Asking the participants in such a conversation to articulate their experiences will bring to the fore the irreducible singularity that is the hallmark of all experiences.

Bibliographical Essay

The formative power of narrative has been a staple of popular anthropologies; for one of the latest exemplars, see Yuval Noah Harari, *Sapiens: A Brief History of Mankind* (New York: Vintage, 2024). The most comprehensive and sophisticated version of the argument for the foundational power of narrative is by Albrecht Koschorke, *Fact and Fiction* (Berlin: de Gruyter, 2018). For the realism of Don Quixote, see José Ortega y Gasset, "Meditations on Quixote," in *Theory of the Novel: A Historical Approach*, ed. Michael McKeon (Baltimore: Johns Hopkins University Press, 2000), 271–316. For the narratological structure of Western novels, see Franz Stanzel, *Theorie des Erzählens* (Göttingen: Vandenhoeck & Ruprecht, 1995)—still well worth translating—and Mieke Bal, *Narratology: Introduction to the Theory of Narrative* (Toronto: University of Toronto Press, 1997). For an influential account of the bildungsroman tradition, see Franco Moretti, *The Way of the World: The Bildungsroman in European Culture* (London: Verso, 2000). See also the important late essay by William James, "The Experience of Activity," in *Writings 1902–1910* (New York: Library of America, 1988), 805; for the context of this thought, see Jeremy Dunham, "The Experience of Activity: William James's Late Metaphysics and the Influence of Nineteenth-Century French Spiritualism," *Journal of the History of Philosophy* 58, no. 2 (2020): 267–291. For free indirect discourse, see Dorrit Cohn, *Transparent Minds: Narrative Modes for Presenting Consciousness in Fiction* (Princeton, NJ: Princeton University Press, 1984) and Ann Banfield, *Unspeakable Sentences: Narration and Representation in the Language of Fiction* (Routledge, UK: Oxford, 1982). Neither Cohn not Banfield relate the emergence of free indirect discourse to the industrialization of the novel in the nineteenth century. For the relation between free indirect discourse and censorship that became the center of Flaubert's trial for obscenity, see William Olmsted, *The Censorship Effect: Baudelaire, Flaubert, and the Formation of French Modernism* (New York: Oxford University Press, 2016), 14–40. For the continuing importance of free indirect discourse, see Timothy Bewes, *Free Indirect: The Novel in a Postfictional Age* (New York: Columbia University Press, 2022).

The concept of "pseudofactual" representation for the editor in fiction is used to brilliant effect by Nicholas Paige in *Before Fiction: The Ancien Régime of the Novel* (Philadelphia: University of Pennsylvania Press, 2011). For the cultural value of "having read," see Paul Guillory, *Cultural*

Capital: The Problem of Canon Formation (Chicago: University of Chicago Press, 1995). The value of having "an" experience as provided by works of art is in John Dewey, *Art as Experience* (New York: Penguin, 2005), 36–58. The quote from R. D. Laing is from his astonishing book, *The Politics of Experience and the Bird of Paradise* (Harmondsworth, UK: Penguin, 1967), 16.

Coda: Singularity, University, Experience

The preceding chapters have explored three dimensions of the phrase "reading experiences": they have tried to read experiences in their metaphysical and historical dimensions in the West; they have claimed that in the encounter with novels we read others' experiences; and they have sought to show that reading makes experiences and thus reaches beyond decipherment and intellectual absorption. This exploration sought access to the openness and potentiality, the essential novelty of experience that dims and diminishes as we are asked to distinguish and judge.

In many Eastern cultures, but also in some Western contemplative traditions, this access is maintained through meditation techniques that encourage practitioners to detach from their experiences, particularly from the narrative form they have acquired, and to sever, even if only temporarily, the affective ties that make an experience "mine." Other outcomes of one's experience are possible, other views and reactions to events than those dictated by prejudice and habit. The therapeutic goal is to increase a personality's amplitude, the tolerance not just for others' struggles with their experiences but for one's own.

Most meditation cultures have a rich record of oral or written examples that show practitioners how others have dealt with such experiences as duty, grief, desire, anger, anxiety, or sluggishness. For historical and philosophical reasons outlined in previous chapters, such a record of experiences is available in the Western tradition in the modern novel as it emerged in the seventeenth century. It does not matter, from this perspective, that these are "fictitious" experiences as long as they carry the characteristic attributes of temporal extension and the potential to develop otherwise.

The meditative work, undeclared though it may be, is accomplished in the reading, itself a temporally extended experience that follows a character's experience from the removed, "meditative" distance afforded by the novel's form and conventions. This reading has the freedom to entertain other possibilities of experience, be they the ones the characters make or the ones the reader would make in their its stead. It may not yet be critical reading, but in its reflectiveness it is also not submerged in emotion and affect, and it is probably what motivates most readers to read prose fiction.

The remarks in this coda reflect on how this experience can be integrated into the academic teaching of literature. There are, of course, other ways to discuss narrative literature; in the Anglo-American tradition, dedicated review journals give critics much greater liberty to situate their reading in personal experiences, even if these are most often other reading experiences. I have participated in book clubs with "lay readers" and enjoyed them tremendously; but clubs don't typically keep a record of their conversations.

The principal question, however, is whether and why this dimension should be included in academic teaching in the first place. I see three reasons, which I list in the order of their importance to me. The first is the dramatic decline in enrollment in courses on literature, in any language, and the fall in the number of majors and minors who consider majoring in a literature department. It is true that enormous economic and social forces exert pressure against the study of any humanistic subject; but it also true that we as scholars and teachers of literature have not done the best job of convincing students and parents of the use value of our subject. In fact, the very idea of assigning utility to the study of literature offends some of its practitioners. They uphold the ideal of precision in reading to which students have to be lead, or of hermeneutic "truth' that emanates from the works. Others argue that reading novels helps us gain knowledge, but to many students it is not clear what kind of knowledge that is and how it relates to the subjects they study in other classes, and to their lives. The inclusion of experience as a dimension of reading as well as a first approach to interpretation both answers the dreaded question of utility—gaining distance to one's experiences is an extremely valuable social skill—and lowers the entrance threshold into the world of novels.

The second reason relates to the theme of the invisibility of experience that has come up repeatedly in previous sections: "I cannot experience your experience. You cannot experience my experience. We are both invisible men. All men are invisible to one another." To R. D. Laing's pithy analysis, the previous pages, prompted by the thought of Nāgārjuna, have added another dimension: we are invisible to ourselves. We rarely see our experiences *as* experiences, as possible steps outside the limits of our habitual actions and reactions. In this double invisibility we encounter the deepest level of diversity in the classroom—in our experiences we are not only different from one another but different from ourselves. Focusing on the experience of reading acknowledges these differences while urging us to bring our experiences to language so that we, and others, can reflect on them. In true empiricist fashion, we are ascending from difference to communication rather than descending from identity— "Let's all share our individual experiences!"—to difference. The notion that in the previous pages has designated this ineradicable difference that we want to respect but bring into communication is singularity. The ideal of a classroom focused even only for a short span of time on the exchange of reading experiences is the ideal of a university of singularities, and it is one that the teaching of literature affords, with the added benefit that we can both do and reflect on this difficult work.

The third reason relates to William James's observation that what we perceive as gaps in our experiences is in fact a lack of attention to conjunctions and disjunctions, to the experiences of "with, near, next, like, from, towards, against, because, through, for, my" (*Pure Experience*, 1161). Writers such as Johann Wolfgang von Goethe, William's brother Henry James, even such austere stylists as Samuel Beckett have closed these gaps, brought experiences closer (*dichter*) together, found meaning in the particles. A look at the Nobel Prize winners in Literature of the last ten years or at the *New Yorker*'s list of best books of the year shows that contemporary novels continue this work with unabated energy and thus ensure the relevance and relative popularity of this once wayward genre.

It is this granularity of attention that characterizes (with other properties) poetic language. When we exhort students to be attentive to the singular in their accounts of their reading experiences, we urge them to come closer to, indeed to practice, poetic language. As scholars, we eschew (for the most part, but with notable exceptions) in our work any intimation of poetic expression so as not to collapse the critical distance; there is no reason why young readers should have to do the same. In my observation, as knowledge-focused teachers of literature we are losing the students who respond to experiences artistically to creative writing, art practice, and media studies; a shift toward greater freedom of expression in the classroom might bring them back (and only mildly disturb the students we have gained from philosophy during the theory years).

I want to repeat a proviso that has been made numerous times in the preceding pages: I am not proposing a paradigm shift or a conversion; I do not advocate for a retreat from critical reading practices or from philological approaches. This would not only contradict all the work I myself have done, it would also invalidate the analysis here proposed—forays into the history of the novel, into the practices of reading, into the history of philosophy are not possible without relying on the methods of critical scholarship. My suggestions, therefore, are only asking to give the experiential level of reading a bit of space. Many colleagues begin their classes with a few minutes of mindfulness practice;

fifteen minutes of conversation about the reading experience would follow nicely after that.

The most important tool in the experience of novel reading is the reading journal. From the outset, teacher and students should keep such a journal and make it available on a teaching platform, anonymously if they so wish. The prompts for these journals have to be precise enough to guide students away from generalities and from quick professions of taste or emotions. Where did you read? On what medium? At what intervals? Did you feel drawn into the story? If yes, by what means did the writer achieve that; if not, what prevented you from getting into it? At what point did you feel enough suspense that you wanted to know how the story developed? Did you feel bored? If yes, what kind of boredom did you feel—impatience with the way the characters acted, annoyance with the writer's style, or with the story itself? Do you know what motivates the characters? Do the characters know? Where could they have gone in a different direction? Do the characters understand the other characters?

Students should be reminded that at this stage they should pay attention to, and try to name, without judging, the resistances the text offers them. *You* are reading this novel: generalities and summaries have no place here; you are *reading* this novel: pay attention to the process, to the change in your attitude to the work and to characters. Questions like these, tailored to the individual novel and its parts, urge readers to dissolve the solidity of representation into the potentiality of experience—to reflect on the multiple roads not taken by a character, or by the author.

At the time of this writing, AIs still acknowledge that they are not making experiences when they read. Like the apostles, they decipher what has been written and seek to make literal or even metaphorical sense of their testamentary reading. They read novels like everything else: as something to know, to categorize, to conceptualize, and to transmit. They do not read like Mary, with all her body, full of hope for a transformational experience.

This makes the conversations about reading experiences as they are outlined in this essay immune to the cooptation by AIs, in particular if they are conducted synchronously.

At the same time, AI tools can free the space and time that once was reserved for the extraction, communication, and testing of knowledge and lead to deeper reflections on the nature of experience and its singularity. If we are prompting students to set aside their rush to judgement and to attend to the experience of reading, we should also encourage them to prompt an AI so that they can find the limits that separate the generality, the common place to which they sometimes gravitate, from the singularity of their own encounter with this book. Conversations with AIs, if conducted in a probing manner and with an open mind not afraid of being challenged by a nonsentient intelligence, can be extremely helpful in highlighting and shedding the artificial—Nāgārjuna would say the conventional—elements in our own ways of reading and judging literary texts. Feeding reading experiences into an AI, as I have done with the examples here published, and asking for editing help quickly brings us to the point where we are forced to reflect on what makes our reading experience a *human* experience—its situatedness, its rhythm, its halo of feelings—and what makes it a human *experience*. Students should be allowed to articulate their experience in media and formats other than the written journal entry. Videos, still images, even music—if they can be brought into the conversation, they should be part of the poetic responses. Self-grading or un-grading seem natural ways to assess experiences that are by definition incompatible.

It is difficult for us as teachers to imagine that students can learn without our physical presence. There is near-universal disapproval of MOOCs and other forms of remote learning, especially in the humanities, and the digital learning platforms that have evolved during and after the COVID-19 pandemic are seen as patches rather than as advances. And yet, for the purpose of bringing the experiential side of reading into focus for students, I have found digital platforms and remote forms of teaching enormously helpful, so long as they include some form of synchronous interaction. After all, the articulation of experiences is not first and foremost a collective activity; it needs time to develop, and on a fundamental level, these articulations cannot be right or wrong, they cannot be debated. If anything, they can be critiqued in the way art classes collectively critique students' work. Moreover, digital interactions may ease the discomfort of students who are reluctant to speak in class, in particular about a topic that may seem private to them. The fact that these interactions can happen outside the classroom may alleviate the concerns of teachers who fear that the inclusion of experiential perspectives will consume too much of their teaching time.

For all of these modifications, the experiential study of literature needs the support of the institutions in which it is situated: departments need to acknowledge experience-based teaching, research in tenure files, and in annual evaluations; universities have to accommodate new formats of teaching and new modes of grading; professional organizations must adjust their standards of excellence so that experiential teaching and learning can find its proper place in the plethora of approaches.

One of the biggest difficulties in this endeavor is the lack of examples. How can one show students what an experiential record of reading actually looks and sounds like—how it differs from a confession, criticism, or emotional judgment? There are, as mentioned, reviews in dedicated journals or newspapers that eloquently discuss the experience of reading, but these are seasoned readers drawing from a lifetime of reading. The paucity of examples is largely a structural difficulty: there can be no examples for singular endeavors. This also means that originality or exhaustiveness cannot be their criteria; indeed, as is the case when someone tells us their dreams, there may be a certain dullness or incoherence about such accounts. Nonetheless, we hope to collect examples at the website thenovelexperience.org.

The teaching of literature has changed greatly in the last decade—there is much more interaction in the lecture hall and in the seminar room, various media are employed, and assignments are often highly imaginative. And yet I think it is fair to say that the emphasis in most formats is still on knowledge—knowing a text and its author, the historical circumstances of its emergence and its success, its representational techniques, the work of identity and positioning it performs, and its reception.

By integrating the dimension of experience into the teaching of literature, we create a richer, more inclusive, and more dynamic academic environment, we open our work up to the reading public at large, and we begin the dialogue with Artificial Intelligences that will come to us one way or another. This approach not only addresses pressing challenges, such as declining enrollment, but also nurtures deeper engagement, encouraging students to see reading as both a personal and communal act of discovery. In doing so, we reaffirm literature's relevance as a field where the complexities of human experience are not just studied but lived.

Bibliographical Essay

For the very different Western tradition of philosophical meditation as conversion and as a means to find first causes, see Christopher Wild, *Descartes's Meditative Turn: Cartesian Thought as Spiritual Practice* (Stanford, CA: Stanford University Press, 2024), 1–16 and 187–221. A surprising conjunction of Buddhist wisdom and critical reading practices is articulated by bell hooks, *Teaching to Transgress: Education as the Practice of Freedom* (London: Routledge, 1994), 14. A wonderfully rich account of the emotional attachment we form to works of art and to characters in novels is by Rita Felski, *Hooked: Art and Attachment* (Chicago: University of Chicago Press 2020). For the distinction between "lay" and "professional" readers and its historical and institutional context, see John Guillory, *Professing Criticism: Essays on the Organization of Literary Study* (Chicago: University of Chicago Press, 2022), 318–342. For the notion of singularity in the context of Western concepts of individuality and identity, see Samuel Weber, *Singularity: Politics and Poetics* (Minneapolis: University of Minnesota Press, 2021), 1–12.

Acknowledgments

Research and writing for this book was supported by a fellowship from the Center for Humanities and the Arts at CU Boulder in the Spring of 2022 and a sabbatical leave from the College of Arts and Sciences in the fall semester of 2024. It condenses two conversations about the relation of literature to experience: the first, with Paul Fleming, now extends into its sixteenth year; the second, with Greg Laugero, to almost 18,000 miles. They have challenged me on hard climbs, waited at the top, and tempered my occasional overconfidence on descents. I thank the tetrarchs of my German-speaking world, Peter Geimer, Eva Geulen, Ralph Ubl, and Joseph Vogl, for listening and not abandoning me in these perilous times. Jeff Cox and Ann Schmiesing demonstrate every day that high administrative office at CU Boulder and deep commitment to humanistic scholarship are indeed compatible. Ed Dimendberg steered the book to port with his legendary expertise. Alison Cool provided wisdom and beans, and Anastasiya Osipova showed the warmth and brilliance that come from braving difficult circumstances. We will all have to learn this. Rick Wells always knows where to travel next. Deborah Hodges Maschietto allowed me to look at the Palazzo Spini Feroni for a whole month. Without Serafina and Jenna, none of this would have been possible.

www.ingramcontent.com/pod-product-compliance
Lightning Source LLC
Chambersburg PA
CBHW021404090426
42742CB00009B/1005